A MAN NAMED
SMITH

Published in the USA by:
BearManor Media
PO Box 1129
Duncan, Oklahoma 73534-1129
www.bearmanormedia.com

978-1-59393-528-3

Printed in the United States of America.
Cover Design by Sue Slutzky
Book design by Brian Pearce | Red Jacket Press

A MAN NAMED SMITH

THE NOVELS AND SCREEN LEGACY OF THORNE SMITH

ANTHONY SLIDE

TABLE OF CONTENTS

The Supernatural – Sex – Pornography – Prostitution – F. Anstey – Alcohol and Prohibition – Herbert Roese – Nudity – Underwear and Lingerie – Females – Homosexuality.

CHAPTER ONE

Early Years – Dorothy Parker – *Biltmore Oswald: The Diary of a Hapless Recruit* – *Out o' Luck: Biltmore Oswald Very Much at Sea* – The Thorne Smith Dogs – "Yonder's Henry" – The Thorne Smith Cats – *Haunts and By-Paths and Other Poems* – Harold Stearns and *Civilization in the United States: An Inquiry by Thirty Americans* – Free Acres – *The New Yorker* – *Dream's End* – *The Stray Lamb.*

CHAPTER TWO

Did She Fall? – *Topper* the novel – Roland Young – *Topper* the film – *Topper Takes a Trip* novel and film – *Topper Returns* – *Topper* on radio and television.

CHAPTER THREE

Ogden Nash – *The Night Life of the Gods* the novel – *Night Life of the Gods* the film.

CHAPTER FOUR

Turnabout the novel – *If I Were You* – *Turnabout* the film – *Turnabout* on television.

ACKNOWLEDGEMENTS

As a teenager, growing up in the British industrial city of Birmingham, this author was an avid reader of the novels of Thorne Smith. The sexual situations and the nudity were pleasantly arousing, and far removed from my personal life and other literary works I was encouraged to peruse. With the passing years, my tastes in literature changed, hopefully for the better, and it is only now, with the imminent approach of old age (or is it already here), that I return to my childhood hero, and attempt to analyze his writings and his contribution to the world of film and television. It is perhaps too late to revive my youthful appreciation of Thorne Smith; as one modern commentator has observed, "He should be read when young."

In my endeavors, I have been helped, as always, by the staff of the Margaret Herrick Library of the Academy of Motion Picture Arts and Sciences. At the Doheny Memorial Library of the University of Southern California, I had the welcome assistance of John Ahouse, curator of American Literature in its Special Collections Division, and, as so often in the past, Ned Comstock in the Cinema Library and Dace Taub in the Southern California Regional History Center. Without that marvelous website, abebooks.com, I would not have been able to locate Thorne Smith's out-of-print works. Additional out-of-print Thorne Smith volumes were provided by the Literature Department of the Los Angeles Central Library, where I also undertook some further research. In Washington, D.C., Elias Savada was incredibly helpful in checking on the copyright status of Thorne Smith's writings, and also in locating one of the novelist's grandsons. (Unfortunately, the Smith family displayed a marked disinterest in the project.)

I am also grateful to Tim Arnold of the Media Relations/Public Affairs Office of the University of Virginia, Robert Dagg, Wes D. Gehring, Robert Gitt, Howard Green, Jere Guldin, Anne Jeffreys, Marty Kearns, Leonard Maltin, David Marowitz, Tim McHugh, and Jim Pepper.

As with so many of my recent books, I owe a tremendous debt of gratitude to Sue Slutzky for her help in scanning the illustrations, and, here also, for the splendid cover. Brian Pearce served as a brilliant production editor, creating a marvelous design for the interior of the book.

In that Thorne Smith left no papers, anyone writing about the author must, of necessity, rely on one primary source, and that is the 1951 dissertation by Joseph Leo Blotner titled *Thorne Smith: A Study in Popular Fiction*. Dr. Blotner was later to gain prominence as the biographer of two major American literary figures, Robert Penn Warren and William Faulkner. Because Dr. Blotner had access to Smith's two daughters, with whom he had attended high school, and also to letters from Smith to actor Roland Young, the location of which are no longer known, his dissertation serves as a unique Thorne Smith archives. I am extremely grateful to Dr. Blotner for talking with me and for allowing me to freely use his research.

Finally, and as always, I am grateful to Ben Ohmart at BearManor Media for agreeing to publish this book and for his personal enthusiasm for Thorne Smith.

The majority of illustrations in the book are from the author's collection. Others were provided by the Academy of Motion Picture Arts and Sciences. The portrait photograph of Thorne Smith is from the Library of Congress.

Thorne Smith, circa 1930.

INTRODUCTION

The contribution of Thorne Smith to the motion picture and to television is substantial, not only directly through the adaptations of his novels, but also, and equally importantly, in an indirect fashion, because of the manner by which his storylines and characters have influenced a considerable number of Hollywood films and television productions. Thorne Smith may have been "less than great," as Joseph Blotner has written, but his work did lead to a remarkable media phenomenon. If there was a genre with the awkward designation of Comedy-Fantasy or perhaps Comedy-Supernatural, it would be dominated by the novels of Thorne Smith and by their screen adaptations. It might also well include *Here Comes Mr. Jordan*, its remake *Heaven Can Wait*, *Beetlejuice*, *Ghost*, and many other feature films, as well as the television series *Bewitched* and *I Dream of Jeanie*. All have their origins in the writings of Thorne Smith. If Henry James created the 19th Century American ghost, then Thorne Smith deserves credit for giving birth to a much more pleasant, 20th century variety, a practical, modern ghost who has continued to find form into the new millennium.

The supernatural is a dominant factor in the novels of Thorne Smith. Aside from the ghost, as represented by *Topper* and its sequel *Topper Takes a Trip*, there is transformation, as in *The Night Life of the Gods* and *The Glorious Pool*, and there is transfiguration, as represented best by *The Stray Lamb*. It may not always be in the form of a ghost, but the supernatural in one guise or another is represented in almost all of Thorne Smith's novels.

There is nothing particularly alarming or frightening about a Thorne Smith ghost, and the later ghosts based on his formula. To a large extent, they are rather kindly men and women, anxious to help the living, even if the latter are not always enthusiastic about the idea. The supernatural world created by Thorne Smith is one in which the living and the dead live in somewhat frenetic harmony. The terrifying ghostly specter, embodied by Peter Wyngarde, in the 1961 Henry James-inspired film, *The Innocents*, has no relationship to a Thorne Smith ghostly incarnation. The novelist's apparitions are far closer to the vintage cartoon character, Casper the friendly ghost, who made his live action feature film debut in 1995, but, of course, with added nudity and sex.

It may well be argued that there is French farce, of which Georges Feydeau is one of the best known exponents. There is English farce, exemplified by *No Sex Please, We're British*, a title that says it all. And there is Thorne Smith, who may have borrowed in part from his European colleagues, but whose comedic antics are strictly American. Arguably, the European who comes closest in storyline to Thorne Smith is W.S. Gilbert of Gilbert and Sullivan fame. Like Gilbert, Smith creates a Topsy-Turvy world where, as in the song from *H.M.S. Pinafore*, things are seldom what they seem.

There is generally little, if any, logic to a Thorne Smith plotline, just as often there is not very much of the latter beyond a one-joke situation. "Like life itself my stories have no point and get absolutely nowhere," wrote Smith. "And like life they are a little mad and purposeless...Quite casually I wander into my plot, poke around with my characters for a while, then amble off, leaving no moral proved and no reader improved."[1]

Thorne Smith has a one-track mind, focused on the "worst" excesses of alcohol and sex. It is a common track, and one that sometimes is a little too narrow in purpose. Often it appears that a Thorne Smith novel might work equally well, if not better, as a short story.

As Scott Veale has written, "he was intoxicated with non sequiturs and aimless repartee."[2] Rather, Smith breaks the rules of nature and society. Like George Bernard Shaw's Alfred Doolittle in *Pygmalion*, he is railing against middle-class morality. Hedonism might well be defined as his mantra. The characters in Smith's novel do just as they like, as we might like if not shackled by society's mores. What we would not give to converse at length and with pleasure, regardless of the impact of our remarks; to play without concern as to the end result; and to love without thought of the consequences. Thorne Smith would be truly horrified by the "family values" of the 21st Century. Again to quote Scott Veale, "It may be that the insouciant pleasures of Smith's fiction verge on the sinfully quaint in this irony-drenched postmodern era. But one suspects that more than a few readers would find his mischievous spirits and hapless humans awfully good company."

Sex is prevalent in every one of Thorne Smith's novels. And yet there are no four letter words, no explicit sexual acts, and certainly nothing particularly censorable in his descriptions. The actual, the physical, sex exists only in the mind of the reader, who takes what is on the printed page and embellishes it to his or her own satisfaction. For example, in *Skin and Bones,* it would appear that the central character, Quintus Bland and a married couple, the Whittles, engage in group sex. A gunman chases Bland for reasons too complicated to explain, and comments, "I learned all about it in France, during the war. Them Frenchies call it a menagerie a trois — and that was just about what it became after the Whittles and Mr. Bland had finished the second bottle."[3]

Pornography as such is referenced in *Rain in the Doorway,* in which the featured department store boasts an extensive Pornographic Department. There are allusions to *Everyman's Manual of Rape* and *Sex Life of the Flea,* which is perhaps an in-joke intended for Smith's actor friend Roland Young, who wrote a short poem on that subject.[4] However, there is nothing really pornographic in the description of the department or its content, only the response of the hero to the images that he is shown."They don't print any dirtier books than that one," says the hero to a female sales assistant. "Even to be standing together in its presence makes me feel that for all practical purposes you and myself are nine tenths married."[5]

Prostitution is defended in *Turnabout,* in which Tim Willows in the body of his wife Sally outrages the congregation at a church supper:

"...I believe in the legalization of the ancient and honorable profession of prostitution...Many a sweet girl has gone wrong because she was not allowed to become a good, honest prostitute. Do you know that last year 2,540 girls disappeared from their homes? Why, I ask you, why? Why did all those lovely girls disappear from their homes? Because they weren't allowed to become good, honest prostitutes — that is, most of them."[6]

Actor John Barrymore hailed Thorne Smith as "the American Dean Swift." Yet, the author himself apparently had little respect for what he created. He regarded himself as nothing more than a hack writer and, apparently, the income that Smith's books brought in towards the end of his life made little impression upon him.[7] His editor at Doubleday, Doran, Malcolm Johnson tried to explain the Thorne Smith phenomenon:

"They were like no other novels ever written. They sprang, like Moby Dick, out of the soil and the life of America, but their roots were in the earth and not in other books. They were native fairy-tales, but at the same time they were satire of a high order. More than either, they were fun to read and reread. Repetition staled none of their gayety, their perception of the tragedies and absurdities of existence…they were suffused with a kindly magic which enabled the characters and the reader alike to escape for a little from the crushing problems of existence, from the lives of quiet desperation, which, as Thoreau once pointed out in an immortal line, the majority of men and women are destined to lead."[8]

The most obvious, but unacknowledged, influence in the writings of Thorne Smith is the English novelist Thomas Anstey Guthrie (1856-1934), who wrote under the pseudonym of F. Anstey. His first novel, *Vice Versa*, published in 1882, contains elements to be found in Smith's work. It is rightfully argued that all "body swap" plots owe much to Anstey's writings. Anstey makes use of asides, in much the same manner as Smith; at one point, for example, he may apologize to the readers for the grammar of his characters. Like Smith, Anstey writes as much about dogs as about people. In the short story, "Don; the Story of a Greedy Dog," he tells of an animal who uses a variety of tricks to get as much food as he can eat. In "A Canine Ishmael," Anstey tells the sad, short story of a dog who accidentally bites a baby and is thrown out on the street; the tale is told to a complete stranger not by the dog's mistress, as the reader is led to believe, but by the baby, now a grown woman.

Both Anstey and Smith were writers who wrote as much to amuse themselves as their readers, although, as one contemporary reviewer of Anstey's autobiography *A Long Retrospect*, published in America in 1936, noted, Anstey was of an age "when violent complexes and confessions of perversity were not essential to success."[9] Thorne Smith probably delighted in living in a new age which provided fodder for his novels. There are some literary critics who argue, not without credence, that if anything it is not Thorne Smith who should be honored as the basis for so many later novels, films and television series, but F. Anstey. However, no matter that there are antecedents, Thorne Smith is still an original. As Joseph Blotner wrote,

"He used fantasy and humor, elements that are old, but combined them with acute observation, wide-ranging imagination, and his own particular and inimitable talent for whimsy and madness. And finally, he had something which he freely gave to his readers without pretentiousness — the gift of light-heartedness and laughter."

Thorne Smith has been described as the jazz age humorist, but, truth to tell, all of his best known works, excluding *Topper*, were published in the 1930s, long after the jazz age had been replaced by the age of the Depression.

While Susan Sontag in her famous essay on the subject makes no reference to Thorne Smith, it is very obvious that he is a prime American purveyor of "camp." Smith has a camp sensibility in that he is "alive to a double sense in which some things can be taken." "Camp rests on innocence," argues Sontag, "but also when it can, corrupts it." Thorne Smith does exactly that. It just so happens that the novelist wrote his books prior to the origin of "camp," and, equally obviously, Susan Sontag had never bothered to read his work.

Today, there are in all probability few who have read the *Topper* books by Thorne Smith, and nevertheless *Topper* features the most famous of American ghosts. As Stephen Whitlock in the *New York Times* wrote, he is "A ghost that haunts us still."[10]

Yet, while Thorne Smith's writings survive thanks to the heavy printings of his novels in earlier years, his name and his legacy are little remembered. What a depressing experience it is to check out Thorne Smith on the internet — the source of all modern knowledge. There is entry after entry on the actress Courtney Thorne-Smith, but only a handful on the novelist who has the misfortune to share her last name.

The internet does little to aid the researcher in his or her search for information on Thorne Smith. Nor do books, newspaper or magazine articles from the past, published the old fashioned way — on paper. There is so little known about him. And that, coupled with his early death, has made Thorne Smith as invisible as some of his best-known characters. He never sat at the famed Algonquin Round Table; perhaps he was never invited or perhaps he found it all a little too pretentious, but, as a result, he is ignored by those wits and intellectuals that did.

It might be reasoned that his stories and his characters are firmly rooted in the 1920s and early 1930, and that the restraints of that period encouraged a readership to glory in the sexual freedom, the nudity, the easy-going lifestyle, and the boozing that Thorne Smith promoted. His novels take readers into an adult fairyland, a Disneyland, in which alcohol is freely available and the rides generally include a loss of clothing. One 1934 reviewer succinctly summed up the Thorne Smith approach: "He found a pattern that sold — how quickly can one strip one's central characters — and how promptly get them to bed."[11] The Thorne Smith novels provide the reader with an escape from reality, but, ultimately, the reader, like the characters themselves at the book's end, must return to the real world, a serious and dull universe. Cheerful bawdiness is not a 21st Century virtue.

Is there a basic tenet, a standard storyline to Thorne Smith? Paul Di Filippo has argued so, noting,

"a Smith book is almost invariably told from the point of view of a middle-aged, stuck-in-a-rut protagonist, whose life opens up upon the advent of a supernatural agent or miraculous invention without which no action could occur. Authority is mocked and seen as blind and misguided; life is revealed as a precarious mystery trip, exploding the false sense of security striven for by the majority of citizens; hedonism and a pagan libertine existence are experimented with and generally endorsed, even if eventually abandoned in favour of a less strenuous, yet open-eyed and newly catholic lifestyle."[12]

Unlike reality, alcohol never seems to impair Smith's characters. They, and ultimately he, inhabit a world that was to disappear with World War Two. When *The Thorne Smith Three-Bagger* was published in 1943, Joan Kahn wrote in the *New York Times* (March 28, 1943), "To a world of war, Thorne Smith brings a brief, refreshing memory of the days when wine, women and madcap pranks were the natural adornments of a peacetime life and not daydreams to be recalled in moments of rest between slit trenches and factory belt lines." Carolyn See points out that the 1944 publication of Charles Jackson's *The Lost Weekend* forced Americans to realize that alcoholism or even common drunkenness had no appeal. "Smith had been dead for about ten years," wrote See "It's a good thing in a way. The news would have broken his heart."[13]

The stories of Thorne Smith advocate the joy of life. Characters such as Topper, his most famous creation, learn to have a good time. And that is basically what Thorne Smith is promoting with his stories. He will often ridicule marriage and argue in favor of adultery, but always in moderation. As Carolyn See has written, "too much adultery, in his eyes, was almost as boring as marital monogamy, which was, in his eyes, unbearable. He loved nature, mountains, and oceans, or at least his fictional characters did. More than anything else, Thorne Smith yearned after fun."[14]

Yes, there was prohibition in the land, and certainly the Thorne Smith characters are little concerned with it. Some critics have suggested that Smith's novels are a reaction to the restraints of prohibition. Carolyn See has described him as "the literary patron saint of hard liquor."[15] Thorne Smith himself referred to his "alcoholic pen."[16] At the same time, it must be acknowledged that the novels are far more than just a paean of praise to the joys of cocktails and hard liquor. Truth be told, *Skin and Bones* revolves around alcohol abuse. It may be alcohol that unlocks the libidos of Thorne Smith's characters, but those locks were decidedly loose to begin with. It is also very apparent that boozing is best left to the better class of Americans. As Thorne Smith has it in *The Stray Lamb*, "All those who dwelt on the right side of the tracks knew exactly the class of people for whom the Prohibition Act was intended."[17]

The writer himself was no walking advertisement for the pleasures of alcohol. He admitted that if took only one drink of whiskey, he would be drunk for six months. As he recalled for H. Allen Smith, he didn't mind the penalty he had to pay after his long benders, except for one thing. He would be hauled off to a sanitarium in the country, "They'd take me out and stand me up against a brick wall, mother-naked, and they'd turn a fire hose on me. That was a thing I resented bitterly."[18] A whiskey bender, a nude scene and a fireman's hose — it all sounds just like a perfect Thorne Smith scenario!

And there were, undoubtedly, elements of Smith's life that suggest he might well have been a character in one of his own books. Again, H. Allen Smith tells a story of Smith's visiting his publisher's office. He is walking onto Madison Avenue, stops to wave a greeting to a secretary, removes his jacket, and then disappears into an open manhole, complete with a red flag and a "Men Working" sign. A little later, half-a-dozen workmen climb out of the manhole, followed by Smith, who joins them for a sandwich. After lunch is over, and the author has shared the contents of his hip flask, the workmen return down the manhole, with Smith bringing up the rear.[19]

When actor Roland Young told Smith that he was inclined to believe he was only another character out of his books, the author responded, "I often wish I were. They always seem to have a rather merry time of it."[20]

Thorne Smith was not the only member of his family to generate public interest for somewhat unusual behavior. In June 1936, the *New York Times* reported that the novelist's nineteen-year-old niece, Carol Thorne-Smith, had been reported missing by her parents. She had left home with little money and no change of clothing. Two days later, Carol returned home, claiming to have been visiting school friends. A month later, it was revealed, that on February 2, 1936, Thorne-Smith married Thomas J. Linane, the twenty-three-year old son of a local gardener. The marriage was reported to be a surprise to her parents who had no comment.[21]

Nudity is a prominent theme in the novels, usually but certainly not always limited to the ladies of the cast. Yet the nudity is always lacking in detail. Smith never gets into any enthusiastic descriptions of bodily parts. Breasts and genitalia are almost pointedly ignored. Male chests are never identified as hairy or clean-shaven. Women's bodies are generally large or of acceptable size. For all that Thorne Smith does not write, the male body might be no more different to the female. Ultimately, it is the clothing that is intended to titillate the reader not the body that it hides.

The significance of nudity is discussed by the title character in *Topper Takes a Trip*, as he muses that "Instead of holding a series of silly disarmament conferences at which everybody gets hot and bothered and cables home to hurry up with more guns — instead of this, why not institute a set of disrobing conferences…Let us strip ourselves of our all and face each other man to woman instead of man to man." Topper envisages the American ambassador clad only in a pipe, a French politician wearing only a beret, an Italian clad only in a blackshirt, and, of course, Mahatma Gandh "taking everything quite naturally."[22]

In *Turnabout*, a judge ponders on the meaning of "mother-naked," asking, "Do fathers never get naked? Do I understand that they sit about the house all day long muffled up to their ears? Expressions like that exasperate me."[23]

HERBERT ROESE

It was the ladies whose buttocks and breasts would be featured in the illustrations, as well as on the dust jackets, and these are the work of the brilliant but little known Herbert Roese. As one reviewer put it, every Roese must have its Thorne, although were it not for effect the names should be reversed. Thorne Smith might have provided the words, but it was Herbert Roese who brought the female characters in the novels to life for the titillation of a substantial male readership. As editor Malcolm Johnson wrote in 1934, "Mr. Roese has become as closely identified with Mr. Smith as ever Tenniel was with Lewis Carroll. His pictures have mirrored the text with such unblushing fidelity that today a new Smith novel without his pictures would be unthinkable."[24]

While the faces of the ladies were generally well delineated, the bodies would often be little more than a series of well-planned brush strokes. Nipples were seldom to be seen, although the cleavage between both the breasts and the buttocks were well defined. Some of the best and most provocative of the Roese illustrations are those that appear in *Topper Takes a Trip* and *The Bishop's Jaegers*. In addition to Smith's novels, Roese also provided illustrations for at least two other books, both published in 1935, *Strange News* by Alan Griffiths (Doubleday, Doran) and *Ernestine Takes Over* by Walter Brooks (William Morrow). The latter was described by the *New York Times* (February 24, 1935) as "a humorous fantasy in the Thorne Smith vein." In a non-Thorne Smith vein, and in a realistic style, Roese contributed serious cartoons to the *New York Times* for the "Help for the Neediest" Campaigns in 1935, 1936, 1939, and 1940. Active at least through into the 1950s, Herbert Roese was also responsible for a character named "Babe" featured in *Life* magazine

The importance of the Herbert Roese illustrations in selling the novels should not be underestimated. As Frank Luther Mott wrote in his history of best sellers, "Thorne Smith's *Topper* would not have been a winner without its sex appeal and the picture of slightly adorned pulchritude on the cover of the Pocket Books edition."[25]

Thorne Smith, himself, was not initially pleased with Roese's contribution to his novels and went so far as to ask his publisher that the dust jackets be more conservative in design. He wrote to Roland Young, "The artist, a man named Roese, seemed to get the impression that none of my women ever wears any clothes at all. Occasionally they do."[26]

The author himself was no slacker when it came to stripping off. He boasted proudly that he wrote his books wearing the minimal amount of clothing. Stripped to the buff while sitting in the hot sun of Florida or France was Thorne Smith's writing ideal. In a 1933 gossip column in the *Los Angeles Times*, Grace Kingsley described Smith as doing "his writing in the open sunlight as sparsely garbed as the antideluvian author who carved his hieroglyphics on rock." As Smith explained it, while in the Navy he had acquired a combination of flu, pneumonia and pleurisy: "I have never completely recovered...so I like to do my writing in the garden as unfettered with clothing as some of the characters in my books."[27]

One wonders if there is not a narcissistic quality to Thorne Smith's writings in that many of his leading men — Topper is one obvious exception — are usually his age. They are generally more than acceptably good-looking, and they often seem to enjoy losing their clothes and scampering around in the nude.

Underwear features prominently in the novels of Thorne Smith, most notably in *The Bishop's Jaegers* from 1932, whose title probably means nothing to today's readership but refers, in fact, to a pair of long under-pants. The novel opens with descriptions of the principal characters and their underwear, beginning with the aforementioned jaegers:

"To Bishop Waller drawers were merely the first move in a long, grim contest with the devil, a contest in which long grim drawers served as the shock troops of righteousness."[28]

Josephine Duval's undergarments are hardly drawers at all, but "more like a passing thought or an idle moment."[29] Peter Duane Van Dyck never considers his underwear and so accidently puts on one pair over the other. Yolanda Bates Wilmont has a maid to deal with her underwear, "fragile poems done in gossamer and lace — real lace."[30] Former model Aspirin Liz wears "tent-like bloomers." Pickpocket Little Arthur sleeps in his drawers and needs a new pair.

Before long, the principal characters in *The Bishop's Jaegers* have lost their underwear and, through a complicated plot contrivance, end up in a nudist colony. The Bishop is allowed to retain his jaegers; Yolanda strips off only to discover that nobody cares; while Little Arthur discovers there is no call for a pickpocket in a nudist colony. It is a young man named Jones, who runs the nudist colony and who defends nudity, pointing out, "Jean Jacques Rousseau, Havelock Ellis Craft [sic] Ebbing, and even that indefatigable humanitarian, Mr. H.G. Wells, not to mention innumerable other great thinkers…have all at one time or another been preoccupied with the idea of nudity."[31]

The scenes at the nudist camp provide Thorne Smith with the opportu-nity to philosophize on the naked body, white and black, as Peter Duane Van Dyck studies the scene from his window:

"Had the bodies been black instead of white, he would have felt a little better about it. Black bodies and brown ones had a way of getting naked. But, then, the black races were not essentially interested in things of the flesh like the white race. No, black people took the flesh at a stride and passed on to the supernatural and other things of the spirit with only an occasional fleshly picnic — a good rough-and-tumble sort of orgy that cleared up a lot of nonsense and left their thoughts free for other and more important considerations."[32]

(African-Americans are practically invisible in Thorne Smith's world. There is a "negro" servant in the 1934 short story, "Yonder's Henry!," and, the word "nigger" is used twice. However, to criticize Thorne Smith for such usage would practically require the same level of disapproval being addressed to all writers, not to mention filmmakers, of this period. What the stereotypical characterization of the African-American exemplifies is that Thorne Smith and his character live in the stereotypical world of his day, not only inhabited by Negro servants but also by Irish policemen and other examples of racial casting.)

The Thorne Smith women wear attractive underwear, or lingerie. Generally, the most intimate of ladies apparel has the name of "step-ins," a somewhat old-fashioned term. The mischievous Meg in *The Night Life of the Gods* calls them, more appropriately, pull-offs. The Thorne Smith men, no matter their age or good looks, wear "drawers." For example, in *The Stray Lamb*, the handsome boyfriend of the title character's daughter is one of a group who remove their outer garments after a heavy shower; he is reported as "shivering convincingly in his drawers."[33] The underwear-clad gentlemen in Thorne Smith stories probably have never done too much for the female or gay readership. Fetishists of ladies' lingerie, however, have definitely discovered a lasting source for their erotic sensibilities in the underwear-clad females of the novels.

Skin and Bones from 1933 carries nudity one step further, with the central character, Quintus Bland, losing both his clothes and his skin to become a skeleton after "inhaling the potent fumes of a secret chemical fluid with which he had been experimenting."[34] Nudity here is almost exclusively limited to Bland, except for one brief feminine exposure. The novel provides its author with the opportunity, through the commentary of his hero, to discuss male nudity as glimpsed in the Turkish bath of a hotel where part of the action takes place:

"The sight made him feel sorry for the male division of the human race. How, he wondered did men manage to grow themselves into such curious shapes and sizes, billowing out here and jutting in there? And how could nature permit such an unequal distribution of stomachs? Some of the stomachs in that room were larger than their owners. In fact, those stomachs were their owners', or at least nine tenths of them. Mr. Bland decided he would much rather associate with naked women. He was still naïve enough to think of naked women only in terms of beauty. There is perhaps the best way to think of naked women, because when a naked woman is not beautiful she is even more depressing to look at than a man."[35]

Smith described his women as "both carnal and convivial and at the same time straight shooters. That to me is the ideal type." The men are "rare characters," but seldom matching their female counterparts in looks.

To Thorne Smith, "Men seem to be born with conventional ideas. Had there been no fig leaves in the Garden Eve wouldn't have been greatly upset about it, whereas Adam would have made an awful fuss."[36]

It might be argued that Smith is a strong supporter of feminism. While the men in the novels are often sad and lonely types, the women are never without ardent companionship. The Thorne Smith male is often a "little man" in terms of his mental well-being, small because the most prominent female in his life, his wife, has made him such. When the "little man" rebels, it is not a self-generated rebellion but, rather, because of a woman who is not his wife. The central characters in the novels may be men, but the Thorne Smith universe tends to center round women rather than their male escorts. The attitude of Sally Willows towards her husband, Tim, in *Turnabout* typifies the attitude of Smith women to their men: "She had come to regard her husband as being just an animal of the lower order that had been thoughtlessly endowed with the gift of speech and an annoying ability to reason rather trenchantly."[37] At the same time, there is unquestionably a strong feminist agenda in *Turnabout* as the husband in his wife's body learns what it is to be a pregnant woman.

Despite his interest in lingerie-clad ladies, Smith is also a creator of strong female characters, most notably Marion Kerby in the "Topper" novels. In *The Glorious Pool*, both Rex Prebble's mistress and his wife are firm-willed, aggressive individuals. In virtually all of Thorne Smith's writings, it is women who pursue rather than are pursued. Most writers would have acknowledged that a leprechaun can only be depicted as male, but not Thorne Smith in *The Night Life of the Gods*, whose 900-year-old leprechaun is very feminine and can convert the living into stone and vice versa. Smith's women are powerful and usually get their way — and their men. With *Turnabout*, Smith takes the case for strong women to a new level in that he has Sally Willows switch roles and bodies with her husband Tim.

Homosexuality, when found in the novels, is never treated sympathetically, although an argument might be made that Thorne Smith is not overly sympathetic to heterosexuality. In *The Bishop's Jaegers*, there is a surreal scene on board a ferry that is lost in the fog. "I'm only a little ferry," the skipper tells the fog. "Fancy that!" responds the fog in insipid tones. "I thought you sounded queer all alone out there in the fog. You poor dear! Just a little ferry — a pansy, as it were."[38]

The Bishop's Jaegers also contains a curious reference to the head of a nudist colony slapping the hero "too low down on the back."[39] It is something that is not liked at all, particularly as he is as nude as the gentleman delivering the slap.

It is *Turnabout* that offers the most obvious opportunity for gay comedy with its male-female sex change. Certainly, there is some mild humor in the effeminacy that the wife, now a man, embraces. But there is not as much as one might expect and most of it is viewed by supporting characters with singular disapproval. There is one sequence, after the wife, now her husband, accidentally visits the ladies' rest room at the office and discusses the matter with his/her boss, containing some social commentary. "I have no relations with men," thunders the boss, to which comes the reply, "I can't help that…It's your loss, not mine." At the close of the conversation, the husband-wife announces, "Sex makes no difference to me. Man or woman — all the same. I'm practically sexless myself."[40]

The Glorious Pool from 1934 features a typical Thorne Smith example of misunderstood words and phrases. Major Lynnhaven Jaffey owns a collection of rare books, which he describes as his "old and rare." (In *Topper Takes a Trip*, Marion Kerby calls Topper her "old and rare,"[41] obviously a favorite phrase of the author.) A fire in the kitchen brings out the local fire brigade and the Major, who has just stepped out of the shower and is wearing only a towel. He offers to show the firemen his "old and rare." "We've got old and rares of our own," responds the officer. "Why should I look at yours? Is there anything funny about it — you know — anything strange?"

"Of course, I can hardly say until I've looked yours over," replies the Major. "I merely thought you might be interested in comparing items."[42]

Further phallic low humor is provided by the fireman's asking to come in off his ladder "and adjust his nozzle." "My nozzle needs fixing," he explains.[43]

There is definitely something gay about some of the Thorne Smith dialogue and situations, no matter what the writer may have intended. His interest may well have been in scantily-clad females, but there are enough scantily-clad males, albethey determinedly heterosexual, to be found in the pages of his novels.

It is not society which is on trial in the Thorne Smith novels, but what society represents in the form of the establishment. It is establishment thinking and the pillars of the establishment against which Thorne Smith rails. The establishment represents the mundane, and the mundane does not belong in Thorne Smith's world. It is no coincidence that in all of his novels, with the exception of *Skin and Bones*, there is a courthouse scene with a judge failing to see the comic side of the characters and the cases being brought in front of him.

If the stories were to be updated, obviously the drinking would need to be replaced by a little, or perhaps a lot, of harmless drug taking. (There is a reference to cocaine in *Skin and Bones*.) But at the same time much that was restrictive in the 1920s and early 1930s is equally restrained today. Sexual freedom and nudity reached its peak in the 1960s and early 1970s and is now in decline in popular culture. What Thorne Smith's characters got up to seventy or eighty years ago may be juvenile to some, but it is just as outrageous to many Americans today as it was back then.

1. Roland Young and Thorne Smith among Others, Thorne Smith: His Life and Times, p. 23.

2. Scott Veale, "Drinking Gin with the Dead," p. 47.

3. Skin and Bones, p. 268.

4. The poem reads:

> And here's the happy, bounding flea —
> You cannot tell the he from she.
> The sexes look alike, you see;
> But she can tell and so can he.

First published in *Not for Children: Pictures and Verse* Doubleday, Doran, 1930.

5. Rain in the Doorway in The Thorne Smith 3-Decker, p. 500.

6. Turnabout in The Thorne Smith 3-Decker, pp. 321-322.

7. H. Allen Smith, People Named Smith, p. 182.

8. Roland Young and Thorne Smith among Others, Thorne Smith: His Life and Times, p. 4.

9. Paul Jordan-Smith, "A Humorist Remembers Victorian Days and Ways," Los Angeles Times, June 21, 1936, p. B8.

10. Stephen Whitlock, "A Fanciful, Haunting Tale of Influence," p. 18.

11. Undated Kirkus review of The Glorious Pool on file in the Literature Department of the Los Angeles Central Library.

12. Paul Di Filippo, "Smith, Thorne," p. 533.

13. Carolyn See, introduction to Topper, p. xiii.

14. Ibid, p. ix.

15. Ibid, p. x.

16. According to a piece in the Los Angeles Herald Examiner, September 2, 1941, missing its title and filed in the University of Southern California Regional History Collection.

17. The Stray Lamb, p. 54.

18. H. Allen Smith, People Named Smith, p. 180.

19. Ibid.

20. Roland Young and Thorne Smith among Others, Thorne Smith: His Life and Times, p. 12.

21. "Daughter of Broker Missing Seven Days" New York Times, January 16, 1936, p. 7; "Miss Thorne-Smith Back," New York Times, January 17, 1936, p. 3; "Miss Thorne-Smith Wed," New York Times, February 20, 1936, p. 17.

22. Topper Takes a Trip, p. 5.

23. Turnabout in The Thorne Smith 3-Decker, p. 397.

24. Roland Young and Thorne Smith among Others, Thorne Smith: His Life and Times, p. 32.

25. Frank Luther Mott, Golden Multitudes: The Story of Best-Sellers in the United States, pp. 289-290.

26. Quoted in Joseph Leo Blotner, Thorne Smith: A Study in Popular Fiction, p. 101.

27. Grace Kingsley, "Hobnobbing in Hollywood," Los Angeles Times, February 14, 1933, p. A7.

28. The Bishop's Jaegers, p. 1.

29. Ibid, p. 3.

30. Ibid, p. 9.

31. Ibid, p. 225.

32. Ibid, p. 184.

33. The Stray Lamb, p. 181.

34. Skin and Bones, p. 2.

35. Ibid, p. 286.

36. Roland Young and Thorne Smith among Others, Thorne Smith: His Life and Times, p. 17.

37. Turnabout in The Thorne Smith 3-Decker, p. 210-211.

38. The Bishop's Jaegers, p. 152.

39. Ibid, p. 240.

40. Turnabout in The Thorne Smith 3-Decker, p. 306.

41. Topper Takes a Trip, p. 130.

42. The Glorious Pool, p. 96.

43. Ibid, p. 101.

THE BIRTH OF A WRITER

The sea played an important role in Thorne Smith's early life and in the embryonic stage of his writing career. In the charming monograph attributed to Smith's friend, comic actor Roland Young, the editor Malcolm Johnson wrote, "How he came to be an author at all is not very clear. The sea is in his blood, and by rights he should by now be an admiral."[1] James Thorne Smith, Jr. was born at the U.S. Naval Academy in Annapolis, Maryland, on March 27, 1892, the son of a commodore in the U.S. Navy who was supervisor of the Port of New York during World War One. The author's father had also served in the Boxer Rebellion and the Spanish-American War, and in 1871, he had married Florence Skyring. Thorne Smith's great grandfather on his mother's side was, reportedly, Don José Maxwell of Rio de Janeiro, fleet owner and coffee planter, and, so it is claimed, the namesake of Maxwell House Coffee.

In later years, Thorne Smith would enjoy the company of one of Don José Maxwell's descendents, a great-aunt who lived to the ripe old age of 102. The lady and Smith would spend much time drinking port, of which she was particularly fond, while conversing between squawks from her parrot.

It is Malcolm Johnson who recounts the first unconventional, if not fantastical, happening in the young author's life. A few months after Smith's birth, he was "mislaid" by a drunken nursemaid in the Baltimore railway station. "As a result," wrote Johnson, "he has since seldom been able to catch a train or keep an appointment within a radius of at least two days."[2] That event, which contains more than a hint of Oscar Wilde and *The Importance of Being Earnest*, was not as traumatic as the sudden loss of his mother in 1896, and his placement, along with an older brother Skyring (born in 1884 and given his mother's maiden name) with various aunts in Virginia and North Carolina. Shortly before his death, Smith recalled,

"When I was a nipper I led a sort of solitary, dreamlike existence. A dearth of playmates. To compensate for this I used to endow my playthings — mostly stuffed Brownies — with life. Finally I became so batty I actually thought they were alive. When my older brother discovered this secret existence of mine he very thriftily turned it to his advantage. This young devil succeeded in convincing me he had the power to kill my Brownies. And he would do this whenever he wanted a quarter. Whereupon I would run through the house, crying, 'They're dead! They're all dead!' until someone gave me a quarter which in turn I gave to my brother. He would then restore my Brownies to life while I, almost ill with anxiety, would welcome them back from the grave. You can see by this that I was a very simple-minded child.

"…Those early experiences have left their mark with me. Even today I can see more vividly with my imagination than I can with my eyes. I don't quite side-step reality, but I'm inclined to read into it my own meanings; which is not always a wise thing to do. However, I'm just as happy as if I had real good sense."[3]

The young man was subsequently educated at the Locust Dale Academy, a boarding school, in Virginia, St. Luke's preparatory school in Wayne, Pennsylvania, and at Dartmouth College, where he joined the Psi Upsilon fraternity and qualified for the cross country track team. After his sophomore year, Thorne Smith left Dartmouth in June 1912, and embarked on a career in advertising. He also spent time traveling with his father, and, as Joseph Blotner writes, "Despite their constant separation, due to sea duty for the father and school for the son, there existed between the two a deep affection, attested by the dedication of Smith's first serious literary work, *Haunts and By-Paths:* To The Commodore — God Bless Him!"[4]

The two men would stay at the Montowese Hotel in Branford, Connecticut, and there Thorne Smith met Dorothy Rothschild, who would later gain fame as Dorothy Parker. In the winter of 1916, Smith and Parker lived at the same New York boarding house at 103rd Street and Broadway. Smith would spend time in Parker's room, drinking coffee, helping her revise her poetry and making love. It was a very casual affair, and Thorne Smith remains nothing more than a footnote in the biographies of Dorothy Parker. As the lady herself recalled, "We used to sit around in the evening and talk. There was no money but Jesus we had fun."[5]

An acquaintance at the time, John D. McMaster remembers some-what differently,

"Thorne and Dorothy were the wits of the place. Thorne liked his liquor even then, and his jokes were ribald. The highlight of the week came on Sundays, when he and Dorothy and the latter's brother con-ducted a 'Sunday School Class' for the youngsters. They would act out Jonah and the Whale, Potiphar's wife, Daniel in the Lion's Den, Salome, and so on."[6]

It has, of course, been suggested that Parker may well have been a model for some of Thorne Smith's strong female characters. In that Smith neither acknowledged even his friendship with Parker in any of his writ-ings nor any influence she may have had on him, such an argument appears vacuous.

Certainly, the appearance of Dorothy Parker, the endless early fight against poverty, the Greenwich Village residences, and the untimely early death represent the impeccable credentials for a writer of Smith's genera-tion. As Stephen Whitlock commented in the *New York Times*, "Smith's was the perfect literary life."[7]

BILTMORE OSWALD:
THE DIARY OF A HAPLESS RECRUIT

Smith enlisted in the Navy in December 1917, and was assigned to New York's Pelham Bay Naval Reserve Training School. He was appointed editor of the Naval Reserve newspaper *The Broadside*, "published by the Enlisted Men of the Naval Training Camp, Pelham Park, New York," which he expanded from a four-page to a fifty-page periodical. As well as writing editorials and the occasional poem, Smith created the comic char-acter of a hapless sailor named Biltmore Oswald. In that Smith described himself to a fellow draftee as "the most inept sailor in the Navy,"[8] it may well be that Biltmore Oswald possesses some of his creator's attributes, although he is certainly far less intelligent.

A couple of months after the end of World War One, Thorne Smith left the Navy in January 1919, and began his literary career in earnest. The inspiration for his first two works inside hard covers was Biltmore Oswald. Published by the Frederick A. Stokes Company in 1918 and 1919, the two were relatively short in length. The first, *Biltmore Oswald: The Diary of a Hapless Recruit*, was a mere eighty-seven pages in length.

The second volume, *Out o' Luck: Biltmore Oswald Very Much at Sea*, ran to 120 pages. As with his later and better known novels, both books benefit from the presence of substantial illustrations — here from the pen of Richard Dorgan, also a member of the U.S. Naval Reserve.

The stories, or more precisely diary entries, in both books are reprinted from *The Broadside*. *Biltmore Oswald* follows its central character from February 23 through September 6. Written in a snappy, fast-paced, comedic style, the book begins with Oswald being interviewed by an enlisting officer:

"Do you enlist for foreign service?" he is asked.

"'Sure,' I replied. 'It will all be foreign to me.'"[9]

The novel concludes with Oswald shipping off to regions unknown. In the intervening pages, our hero has been examined in the nude. "Nakedness is the most democratic of all institutions."[10] He has also been persuaded to don female attire to appear as a show girl in an amateur camp production of *Biff-Bang*. "Feminine apparel for me has lost for ever the charm of mystery that formerly touched it with enchantment," reports Oswald.[11] He devoted six pages to the experience, including the matter of having his chest shaved by a barber who describes it as the "bottom part of hees [sic] neck."[12]

OUT O' LUCK:
BILTMORE OSWALD VERY MUCH AT SEA

Out o' Luck: Biltmore Oswald Very Much at Sea is described by its publisher as "A book that every man in the Navy will want as a souvenir of his sea-going days." A more than hopeful desire, influenced by an ever more hopeful yearning for major sales. The book begins on September 7, as Oswald ships out for an unnamed French port. The War ends halfway through the book, which concludes with its hero back in New York. Along the way, Oswald describes golf as "a sort of game indulged in by the so-called upper classes and practically the entire population of Scotland and the Union League Club."[13]

Out o' Luck contains many of the story twists to be found in the later Thorne Smith novels as the wife of a bookmaker offers Oswald a lift in her automobile and takes him to a New York tea room. "A regular Emile Zola sort of a dump."[14] The lady declares her love for Oswald just as her husband Jack appears, along with Oswald's girl friend Polly ("my permanent sweetie"[15]). Polly and Oswald check into a hotel, but after the latter has gone down the hall to take a bath, he returns, with soap in his eyes, to the wrong room. With the imminent return of the husband of the room's occupant, Oswald tries to escape over a window ledge. A duel with guns and with the bell-boys as seconds follows, but only a cow is shot and killed. (A cow also, of course, makes a guest appearance in *The Night Life of the Gods*.) There is later confusion as Oswald meets another amorous young lady who "laughed like a Bacardi cocktail tastes"[16] and with whom he goes riding, but again Polly arrives to prevent further meetings.

The novel concludes on January 5, with Oswald's leaving the Navy. "Before me lies Polly and the girl," comments Oswald. "Which shall it be? I know not. Let the future decide. All I know is that I am just one jump from a pair of trousers that don't flap at the ends...Now I must hasten to sow some jazz weeds."

THE THORNE SMITH DOGS

Aside from Oswald, the central character in both novels is a dog named Mr. Fogerty, whom the former adopts in *Biltmore Oswald*, introduces to the other dogs in camp and allows to sleep in his hammock. "Mr. Fogerty is almost as much of a comfort in camp as mother," writes Oswald.[17] When Oswald ships out for France, Mr. Fogerty remains behind with "a couple of influential yeoman."[18] The novel is, in fact, dedicated in part to Mr. Fogerty, who is obviously as important in its author's life as his Navy comrades:

"Biltmore Oswald and Fogarty," as envisaged by cartoonist Richard "Dick" Dorgan. In the novels, the dog is named Mr. Fogerty.

"To my buddies, an unscrupulous, clamorous crew of pirates, as loyal and generous a lot as ever returned a borrowed dress jumper with dirty tapes; to numerous jimmy-legs and P.O.'s whose cantankerous tempers have furnished me with much material for this book; and also to a dog, an admirable dog whom I choose to call Mr. Fogerty, with apologies to this dog if in these pages his slave has unwittingly maligned his character or in any way cast suspicion upon his moral integrity."

Dogs played an important part in Thorne Smith's life. They are a regular feature of his novels; as Malcolm Johnson wrote, "his books are full of the most beguiling and clumsy dogs, Oscar, Busy, Dopey, a veritable kennel of them."[19] Joseph Blotner has noted that there are seven dogs to be found in the comic novels of Thorne Smith (two more were cut from the manuscript of *Rain in the Doorway*, the published version of which now contains none).[20] *Topper* features a dog named Oscar, "that prince of dogs,"[21] owned by the ghostly Colonel Scott and his equally ghostly mistress, Mrs. Hart, and Smith has written of how he came into being:

"on the lawn of my one-acre estate there is the tallest, wildest grass in all the world. Once I saw the tail of a dog progressing through this grass like a periscope through the waves. This quaint spectacle set me to thinking about a tail without a dog, and a dog without a tail, and legs without a body, and a body without legs and all sorts of odd manifestations. Thus Oscar came into being. I still like him and wish him well."[22]

Busy, the dog in *Skin and Bones* does not become invisible, but, like his owner, inhales some potent chemical fumes and takes to turning into a skeleton on a regular basis.

Of the various animals into which the title character in *The Stray Lamb* is transformed, only the dog is depicted as tolerant and gentle. He is "the most woebegone, flop-eared, putty-footed, miscellaneous assortment of canine maladjustments,"[23] but he is as lovable as it is possible for any dog to be. The chapter in which the dog appears, "Less Than the Dust," is filled with humanity and devoid of typical Thorne Smith comedic antics. In *The Glorious Pool* (1934), the dog is an aged bloodhound named Mr. Henry, who enters the title swimming pool and is rejuvenated as a puppy.

"YONDER'S HENRY"

Henry is also the name of the canine title character in Thorne Smith's only published short story during his lifetime, "Yonder's Henry!," which appeared in the February 1934 issue of *Esquire*. Other writers featured inside as well as alongside Smith on the cover are Ernest Hemingway, John Dos Passos, Lion Feuchtwangler, Ring Lardner, and Irvin S. Cobb.

A bloodhound, Henry takes on legendary proportions as his owner Albert and Albert's wife tell the story's narrator of their fox-hunting exploits in Texas and invite him to participate, only to discover in the story's final paragraphs that the leader of the hunting pack, Henry, is fast asleep, having over-indulged at breakfast. Basically four pages in length, "Yonder's Henry" is mildly amusing, finding whimsy in the notion of fox-hunting in Texas, seen somewhat through an alcoholic blur.

As a small boy in North Carolina, Thorne Smith slept with a large black dog named Zeb, fighting for space with Smith's cousin Almerine. "It was to this audience, the slumbering beast and my small cousin — that I told my first stories and recited my first poems until presently the three of us were asleep."[24]

Thorne Smith's affection for canines even extended to the later dedications in his books. *Turnabout* is dedicated not only to Smith's brother Skyring and his family, but, and just as importantly, to "Pal, a Dog That Served as a Pillow.'

Mrs. Thorne Smith was, apparently, equally fond of dogs. She was involved with the prestigious Westminster Dog Show, and in February 1942, she was the judge of the Manchester Terriers there.

AND CATS

Thorne Smith does not appear to have the same fondness for cats as for dogs, but there is at least one prominent member of the former family to be found in *Topper*. Scollops is the name of Mr. Topper's cat, who is, to all extents and purposes, the poor man's only friend. He had brought her home one evening four years before the story commences, and it is her eyes which fascinate, "the inexplicable, narrowing infinity between two orange-colored slits,"[25] as the feline gets a chapter — the second — all to herself.

To his credit, Smith understands just how a cat might behave. Thus, when Topper abstractedly touches one of Scollops' ears, she with equal abstraction scratches one of his fingers.[26] When Scollops takes over a chair, "Topper's unconscious craving to be loved made him overlook the fact that this was the most comfortable chair in the room and being such naturally recommended itself to Scollops' practical mind. His knowledge of cats was hardly more extensive than his knowledge of women. In some respects Topper was more fortunate than he realized."[27]

HAUNTS AND BY-PATHS AND OTHER POEMS

Thorne Smith's first published poem appeared, he claims, in the *New York Herald*. It was a comic criticism of the then-Secretary of the Navy. As the author recalled, his father shared his views and sent him twenty-five dollars. The *New York Herald* paid him nothing.[28] Later poetic efforts appeared, as noted, in *The Broadside*, in H.L. Mencken's *The Smart Set*, and elsewhere. Eventually, the poetry was collected together in book form under the title of *Haunts and By-Paths and Other Poems*. Frederick A. Stokes published the anthology in 1919, obviously influenced by the substantial sales — in excess of 60,000 copies — of its author's first two volumes. Unfortunately, the audience for Oswald Biltmore failed to demonstrate either financial or critical enthusiasm for Thorne Smith, the poet.

The Springfield Republican (November 9, 1919) noted that the verse "while not strikingly original is pleasantly human and cheerful." The critic in the *Dial* had a similar response,

"There are a few pieces here — as notably 'Sea Song' — which will remain authentic of their maker's genuine, if not strikingly novel, imagery and lilting cadence; there are many passages in which he is fitfully presented; and there is a great deal that might have been written by any not too clumsy apprentice to the poets."[29]

From a modern perspective, it is difficult to find much to admire in what is described as the most notable piece of verse, "Sea Song," the opening lines of which are

There are those who love the reaching plains
And those who love the crags.
And those who love the twilit woods where melancholy Autumn lags
On sad reluctant feet.
And there are those who love the street
Where arc lights sputter in the rain
And traffic lifts a shrill refrain
Where counter currents surge and meet.
But I am not of these.
Such haunts my fancy flees
Out to the sea, the open sea,
The pouring, roaring, soaring sea,
The wind-whipped, tearing, flaring sea,
The sea that never rests.

The Spanish flu epidemic of 1919 hit Thorne Smith almost concurrently with his release from the Navy. The short-term effects of the flu were negligible, but the long-term effects may well have led to his early death. The short-term effect of Thorne Smith's burgeoning literary career was a move to a more intellectual environment, the Greenwich Village Inn in New York, where fellow residents included Sinclair Lewis and John Reed. Also in Greenwich Village, Smith met Celia Sullivan, who, like him, was of Irish protestant descent. The couple eloped to Rye, New York, where they were married in the autumn of 1919.

Unlike the central characters in his novels, there is no hint that Thorne Smith was ever adulterous. In all probability, Celia was a strong character who encouraged her husband's literary career to the extent that she would type up the manuscripts that he wrote in longhand and handle their submission to publishers, at least in the early years.

HAROLD STEARNS AND *CIVILIZATION IN THE UNITED STATES: AN INQUIRY BY THIRTY AMERICANS*

Following the marriage, the Smiths returned to Greenwich Village, to an apartment on Jones Street, and the new husband joined the financial specialist agency of Edward Bird Wilson, Incorporated, where he was hired to write copy for banking clients. One of Smith's neighbors on Jones Street was Harold Stearns, and he asked Smith to contribute a chapter to a volume on contemporary America, titled *Civilization in the United States: An Inquiry by Thirty Americans*. Described as "an adventure in intellectual co-operation,"[30] the substantial, 577-page volume was published in 1922 at five dollars a copy by Harcourt, Brace. Among the other contributors were Conrad Aiken on "Poetry," Ring Lardner on "Sport and Play," H.L. Mencken on "Politics," Lewis Mumford on "The City," Deems Taylor on "Music," and editor Harold E. Stearns on "The Intellectual Life."

Thorne Smith's essay is witty and biting in its survey of an industry in which he was gainfully employed. "What better man for an amusing and accurate essay on advertising?" asked Harold Stearns.[31] Smith describes himself and his fellow workers as "a group of reluctant and recalcitrant creatures that once were men, who, moving through a phantasmagoria of perverted idealism, flabby optimism, and unexamined motives, either deaden their conscience in the twilight of the 'Ad. Men's Club,' or else becomes so blindly embittered or debauched that their usefulness is lost to all constructive movements."[32] Advertising men are divided into two categories, the copy-writer and the solicitor. The former, of which obviously Smith is a member, are "really not bad at heart," while the solicitors are "beyond all hope."[33] In a form of self-defense, Smith argues that "advertising has kept many artists alive — not that I am thoroughly convinced that artists should be kept alive, any more than poets or any other un-American breed; but for all that I appeal to your humanitarian instincts when I offer this fact in support of advertising, and I trust you will remember it when considering the evidence."[34]

Ultimately, Thorne Smith argued against advertising as a career for men such as himself:

"Generally speaking, however, advertising is the graveyard of literary aspiration in which the spirits of the defeated aspirants, wielding a momentary power over the public that rejected their efforts, blackjack it into buying the most amazing assortment of purely useless and cheaply manufactured commodities that has ever marked the decline of culture and common sense…This advertising brotherhood is composed of a heterogeneous mass of humanity that is rapidly converted into a narrow-minded wedge of fanatics. And this wedge is continually boring into the pocketbook of the public and extracting therefrom a goodly quantity of gold and silver."[35]

The essay contains some of Thorne Smith's best writing, profound in its humorous critique of the advertising community. There are no out-of-control characters, no transformations, no supernatural events, and not a hint of nudity or alcoholism is to be found here. Neither absurd nor over-exaggerated, it is simply sophisticated, literate humor at its best. It is little wonder that reviewing the work in the *New York Times* (February 12, 1922), Branders Matthews described Smith's chapter on advertising as "one of the most readable in the book."

Harold Stearns, who was known to his friends as a "picturesque ruin," and Smith remained close, and in later years when, in 1933, the former returned from an extended stay in Europe, he recalled, "He [Smith] and Celia would stake me [at the Albert Hotel, New York] for a week, during which I might get on my feet. Thorne found me an extra shirt or two, and a few pieces of clean underwear — the little things that give a man self respect."[36]

Back in the United States, in 1938 Stearns published what might be considered a sequel to his earlier work under the title of *America Now*. Thorne Smith was, of course, dead, and only six of the original contributors were included in the new work. Smith was replaced by Roy S. Durstine, president of the advertising agency, Batten, Barton, Durstine & Osborn, and, not surprisingly, his essay offers a positive view of advertising.

Harold Stearns died in Hempstead, New York, on August 13, 1943, at the age of fifty-two. According to *Time* (August 23, 1943), his death marked the end of an era in American life. "The era was that in which Americans believed that their own civilization could not be lived in and those who had the courage of their convictions became expatriates." While Thorne Smith did not exactly fit into this category, he was certainly a frequent, and happy, traveler to Europe, but an argument might be made that he sought to change the civilization in which he lived — the United States — through the satire and social commentary in his novels.

FREE ACRES

When Smith's father died on August 23, 1920, his estate was split between his two sons, James Thorne Smith, Jr. and Skyring Thorne Smith. Thorne Smith used his half of the inheritance to finance a 1921 vacation for him and his wife in the South of France and the 1922 purchase of a summer home, with one acre of land, in Free Acres, New Jersey, a community noted for its artistic aspirations and whose residents included James Cagney and MacKinlay Kantor. Free Acres was a social experiment which began in 1910 at the instigation of Bolton Hall (1854-1938). Hall's philosophy has been described as combining a law of love as taught by Jesus Christ, the economic views of 19th Century politician Henry George and the political rights of the people as defined by Thomas Jefferson. A seventy-five acre, wooded community, Free Acres consisted of eighty-five homes whose purchasers owned the building but not the land which was held collectively by the community. Free Acres was basically a summer only community until the Depression led to many homeowners moving there permanently.

Like other residents of Free Acres, the Smiths would spend the summer months there, and the winters in Greenwich Village. After Smith's death, the property at Free Acres remained the family home. The couple had two daughters, Marion Thorne Smith, born on November 4, 1922 and the namesake for the female lead in *Topper*, and June Thorne Smith, born on March 4, 1924.[37] As Joseph Blotner points out, it was "not easy to be the daughters of a well-known dipsomaniac." Both girls suffered "a certain amount of embarrassment."[38]

Thorne Smith at work at Free Acres.

Throughout the 1920s, Thorne Smith and his family barely survived on the income from the father's professional work. In March 1925, he quit Edwin Bird Wilson, Incorporated, and took up another post as a copy writer with Inecto, Incorporated. The new job lasted eight months, and was followed by six months of unemployment. In April 1926, Thorne Smith found a job with the advertising agency, Doremus and Company, which he left in March 1928 to join the William Green Advertising Corporation, where he remained until December of the same year. To quote the hero of his 1927 novel, *Dream's End*, "I was grimly engaged in creating beautiful illusions about various commodities bought, but not needed, by a duped public."[39] If Thorne Smith had any belief in copy writing, it was based on the comment by the boss of that same hero, that Emerson, a great man, "had the heart of a copy editor."[40]

H. Allen Smith reported on an interview with Smith in the 1920s, "I arrived at the Smith apartment in Greenwich Village. It was a gloomy railroad flat in the basement of an old building, and the furnishings were not only nondescript but shabby. As I came up in front of the house Thorne, who had never been interviewed before, popped out of the entrance and greeted me with an embarrassed sort of violence."[41]

THE NEW YORKER

Following his advertising career and prior to determining that he could enjoy a career as a novelist, Smith was briefly employed at *The New Yorker* during the winter of 1929-1930. As James Thurber recalls, he introduced the novelist to editor Harold Ross:

"Thorne Smith, straight out of Wonderland, looked like a cousin of the White Rabbit, and completely befuddled Ross. The editor took him on though — mainly, I am sure, because he had edited a service magazine during World War I... The two men, disparate if there ever was disparity, talked about the *Stars and Stripes* and a mutual acquaintance who had been on the wartime Army *Gas Attack*. Everything went wrong between Ross and Thorne, who once didn't show up for a week. 'You ought to know where he is,' Ross told me. 'He's your responsibility.' I said that Smith was God's responsibility, not mine or any man's. When he finally did appear, Ross said, 'Why didn't you telephone and say you were sick?' Thorne had a lovely answer to that: 'The telephone was in the hall and there was a draft.'"

Ross let Smith go after assigning him to edit a stack of profiles and discovering that he could not use a typewriter. "He sits out there writing on foolscap with a quill pen," Ross told Thurber.[42]

DREAM'S END

As early as 1921, Thorne Smith had been laboring on what was to be his most lasting achievement, the novel *Topper*. But he put it to one side to work on a serious novel, *Dream's End*, which was initially rejected by a large assortment of publishing houses. As a result of the lack of interest in *Dream's End*, the novelist returned to *Topper*, which was taken up by Robert M. McBride and Company, and published on February 13, 1926.

It was Robert M. McBride which eventually agreed to publish Thorne Smith's penultimate novel of the 1920s, far removed from the style of *Topper*. Composed of two parts, "The Birth and Death of a Dream" and "Return to the Salt Marshes," and an epilogue, and appropriately titled *Dream's End*, the novel is very much of its day, a prime successor to the worst works of female British writers such as Marie Corelli or Edith M. Hull. Thorne Smith might display more intellect than his female counterparts, but the extravagant and overwhelming dramatic style is most similar. The novel did not live up to its publisher's extravagant announcement,

"Only once in a decade comes a novel like this! A story that enchants you — as a beautiful dream!

"Simple ingredients — Two women, one of the flesh, one of the spirit, and a man struggling between love and desire. But when you've finished, you say, Oh, what a book! And vow to read it soon again.

"By Thorne Smith — Thorne Smith, who wrote *Topper*, now ready to head the list of first-rate American novelists."

Written in melodramatic fashion, *Dream's End* is also a good example of the stream of consciousness style of writing that Theodore Dreiser exploited. Unfortunately, it does not owe anything to Dreiser in terms of either quality or appeal. There is nothing here to hold the reader except perhaps a wonder at where the novel will end, but even there, it is doubtful that most readers at the time or since could care. The sordid passion that Thorne Smith has tried to create is simply unrealized, despite a love triangle that should have evoked sexual tension. The hero's swimming out to an island beyond the marshes is as dull as it sounds.

The most interesting, and unusual, part of the novel is neither dissolute nor thought-provoking, but consists of a Bambi-like fairy tale told on the beach to a group of children by the hero. It is the story of a deer who adopts the child of a woodsman who has killed her own child. In time, the child becomes a woman and marries the Lord of the North. When he shoots her deer-mother with an arrow, she leaves him to return to the herd, where she has his child. The child's mother is accidentally killed by the Lord of the North, but their child returns with him to live happily ever after. Reading this story, it is no surprise that Thorne Smith should have attempted a book for children, *Lazy Bear Lane*, published in 1931.

Dream's End is the story of its narrator, David Landor, twenty-five years old, and, like his creator, a copy writer. Viewing New York as "a huge, sponge-like creature implacably bent on absorbing my identity,"[43] Landor accepts an invitation from an elderly artist friend, Hugh MacKellar, to stay with him at his cottage by the sea and the sea marshes. Here, he meets model Scarlet, who tries to seduce him, and Hilda Elliott, the wife of a dissolute and mentally unbalanced neighbor, with whom David falls in love. "My God, the women I've seen and the women I've wanted! The dreams I've had and the songs I've Heard," proclaims David.[44] The community reads more like something that might be found in the Deep South than in New England, where it is presumably located. After much soul-searching and swimming, and a great deal of description of the marshes and the sea, David realizes that Hilda is an abused wife, but fails to save her from her husband's wrath. David returns to the marshes and to his past after Hilda's death. MacKellar and Scarlet are still there, as is Hilda's husband, John. John and Scarlet are now married. The child, Natty, to whom Landor had told his fairy tale, is killed by John Elliott, who dies as his house burns down. The novel concludes with Landor's unexplained death, which is viewed as a beginning rather than an end. The final words that the copy writer turned poet commits to paper prior to his passing are:

"And now the storm is past

I shall sing him upward from death."

Luckily for the author, the new decade was to give him much to sing upward, although ultimately, before it was even half over, it was to witness the end of his brief life.

Dream's End was a success neither with the critics nor the public. The *Saturday Review of Literature* (April 23, 1927) described the work as "a wallow of fevered flapdoodle." The reviewer in the *New York Herald Tribune* (April 10, 1927) could not help but compare Smith's new work to Topper:

"By means of a great deal of description of wild salt marshes and of the mad moods of sea and sky and so-called human beings, Mr. Smith has been at great pains to create an atmosphere which will make credible the unearthly experience of David Landor. For all his labor, however I never felt at home in the story; the illusion was never complete.

"Mr. Smith's spiritualism is more convincing when he takes it lightly, as he did in *Topper, an Improbable Adventure*."

The critic in the *New York Times* (April 27, 1927) was relatively kind, noting that,

"Mr. Smith has written a novel that in subject and style is seldom represented in our contemporary fiction. It is a pretentious flight. It is a gesture in the direction of the stars in which we find the flight to have been successful only in aspiration. Scattered here and there are bits of star dust that have been brushed down in passing, but the general intention seems to have widely missed the mark.

"Mr. Smith has chosen to tell a 'spiritual melodrama' of the conflict of the ideal and desire. He has adapted impressionism to render a psychological travail. He has wavered between projecting character and symbols. Apparently he has found the symbolist poets attractive and desired to make use of their values. In the main, his pattern has been taken from music. *Dream's End* is a symphonic novel. The troubles that arise are in the scoring of the orchestration. It is underscored; the themes do not develop; they remain vague and fumbling threads that never soar to clarity...Mr. Smith has written with a great deal of fine feeling — beauty of words — flashes of remarkable insight; but his vision is never articulately revealed. He has excellent talent and we wish him better luck next time."

Thorne Smith would later joke, "*Dream's End*, my first serious novel, done years ago, is considered by many my funniest. I don't speak to these people, though."[45] The novel did, however, have its admirers. At the time of his death, a columnist in the *Los Angeles Times* urged his admirers to read *Dream's End*, "which never had the success it deserves."[46] A year earlier, in August 1933, Robert M. McBride had reissued the novel, presumably counting on its author's continuing success with comic literature to boost sales.

THE STRAY LAMB

The decade ended for Thorne Smith with a return to the supernatural comedy of *Topper* with *The Stray Lamb*, published in September 1929 by the Cosmopolitan Book Corporation, better known for the magazine of the same name for which it was responsible. "For several years I had to live with the idea of *The Stray Lamb* bussing in my brain before I could find a publisher generous enough to enable me to write it," wrote Smith. "To Joe Antony of the defunct Cosmopolitan Book Corporation I shall be eternally grateful."[47]

A healthy advance from Cosmopolitan enabled Smith and his family to rent a house in Nice on the French Riviera, with a villa next door occupied by the exiled Caliph of Turkey, his eight wives, assorted children and grandchildren and a large retinue. *The Stray Lamb* was completed in Nice and mailed to Cosmopolitan while the Smith family went on a tour of Europe.[48]

The Stray Lamb, for which Thorne Smith claimed to have the idea stuck in the middle of traffic while crossing Fifth Avenue, is the relatively short story of stockbroker T. Lawrence Lamb, transformed into various animal forms by a "little russet man," anxious to save Lamb from the strain of respectability. Lamb becomes a horse (which is the lengthiest and most entertaining transformation), a seagull, a kangaroo, a goldfish, a dog, a cat, a lion, and a combination animal with the head of a rooster, the body of a prehistoric monster and the tail of a lizard. The last apparition takes place in court as Lamb is being sued for divorce by his wife, nicknamed Sapho (not Sappho). A lingerie model with the more plebeian name of Sandra is named as co-respondent. The other main characters in the story are Lamb's daughter, Hebe, who is supportive of both her father and Sandra, Hebe's boyfriend, Mel Long, and Leonard Gray, who appears in amateur dramatics with Sapho and may or may not be in a relationship with her.

Thorne Smith does not make it clear who exactly the Russet Man is, but one critic, Michael D. Walker, has suggested that he is a leprechaun. Walker goes on to note that one of Smith's favorite books was the Irish fantasy novel by James Stephens (1880-1950), *The Crock of Gold*, published in 1912.[49] Certainly, Smith would have been intrigued by Stephens' novel which finds humor in imprisonment of human intellect by various members of society, such as lawyers, doctors, priests, and academics. The difference between the two writers is, of course, that Stephens, who physically resembled a leprechaun, made use of Irish legend and folklore in his stories, whereas Smith created American legend and folklore with his.

Lamb's animal transformations are treated with remarkable equanimity both by Lamb himself and his friends and relatives. Aside from trying to kill him while he is a goldfish, and some might argue with good cause, even the wife is relatively tolerant. *The Stray Lamb* is not a major Thorne Smith effort, and yet it is one of the more appealing of his novels. As the critic in the *New York Times* (November 3, 1929) wrote, "*The Stray Lamb*, with all its hilarity and fantasy, is a wise and tender tale beneath the glitter of its bizarre style. It has a hearty longing for the good things of the world and spirit." The critic for the *New York Herald Tribune* (November 24, 1929) described the novel as "a giddy blend of extravagant nonsense and shrewd wisdom. He [Thorne Smith] erects a tall tower of absurdities on which to swing his sage observations of the social scene and then clambers, monkeywise aloft and throws down his cocoanuts to us. The process is hilariously entertaining to watch and the fruit he tosses down is sound and sweet."

Nobody suffers as a result of what takes place, and, ultimately, all ends well, with Lamb and his lingerie model, along with Mrs. Lamb and her lover Leonard Gray, and Hebe and Mel, all bound for Europe on the same liner. Naturally, the novel concludes as readers of Thorne Smith would appreciate with Hebe's scuttling away at her father's behest to discover if the bar on board is open. The ending indicates that Mr. Lamb has gone through a series of animal transformations, which, ultimately, have lead to his real-life transformation.

At least one commentator has observed that the previous life lead by Mr. Lamb provides him with the means to adopt a new one. Wealth earned in a repressive society is of great help in escaping from such a world. Thorne Smith "wants to say, 'Throw off mundane considerations and live for the joy of the moment'; but, as with everything else, he shows that it is easier to do this if one is already rich."[50] Like all of Smith's male protagonists, Mr. Lamb is wealthy enough to survive any change in his lifestyle. Of course, Mr. Lamb and his creator have something in common in that both lead a humdrum existence in the United States, and both crave for a freer lifestyle in Europe, and particularly in France.

A librarian named Blanche A. Gardiner at the Los Angeles Central Library reviewed the novel for acquisition, and rejected it as "Unnecessary," adding that its effect on the reader was "puzzling" and that it was of interest to "Very few" men, women, boys or girls. She continued, "This satirical jumble is a mixture of *Gentlemen Prefer Blondes*, *Crazy Fool* and *Alice in Wonderland*...A ridiculous yarn, but too frank in spots to be read by the young patron asking for Impossible stories."

The Stray Lamb was the first of Smith's novels to be acquired for the screen, although, in fact, it was never filmed. Actor Roland Young obtained a copy of the novel, and, after an enthusiastic reading, took it to his friend and fellow actor, John Barrymore (to whom many have commented that Thorne Smith bore a close resemblance). In turn, Barrymore invited brother Lionel to come listen to a reading, with his playing all the roles. John Barrymore subsequently purchased the screen rights for $3,000.00.

Barrymore retained ownership of the rights, and, after his death, these rights were acquired by James Cagney and his producer brother Bill.

Initially slated to play the title character was Bob Hope, and there was also some discussion of Cary Grant in the role.[51] Frank Capra was at one point suggested as director.[52] Some years later, Cagney had the notion that he would play the Russet Man and that Robert Montgomery would be Mr. *Lamb*. Nathaniel Curtis adapted the novel, and Britisher Richard St. John was signed to direct. However, a major studio strike in 1947 closed down production only three weeks before the film was scheduled to begin filming. Cagney revived the project again in 1955, planning to film it with his own production company after completion of *Love Me or Leave Me*, in which he co-starred with Doris Day. Again, the project never came to fruition.[53]

It has been suggested by a least one writer that *The Stray Lamb* provided the idea for the popular, and juvenile, Universal series of "Francis the Talking Mule.[54] Interesting as is this hypothesis, it should not be forgotten that when Mr. Lamb becomes a horse, he may think as a human but he does not have the ability to speak. If "Francis the Talking Mule" has an antecedent, it is the short story by F. Anstey, "The Talking Horse," first published in book form in 1892. It is an amusing tale of a gentleman who hires a horse to ride in London's Hyde Park and discovers that the horse can speak, often in quite uncomplimentary and patronizing terms to its rider. The horse persuades the gentleman to purchase him, to find high-class accommodation and to treat him as an equal. Eventually, the horse is responsible for losing the owner the love of his life, is savagely beaten, but throws and seriously injures the gentleman. Here is a story which would have delighted Thorne Smith, and, again, demonstrates the similarity in style between him and F. Anstey.

Another suggestion, by Michael D. Walker, is that elements of *The Stray Lamb* may have found their way into the 1935 James Whale-directed feature film, *Bride of Frankenstein*. Walker posits that just as the half-witted man in the novel befriends Mr. Lamb and vainly tries to fend off the angry villagers, so does the hermit in the film on the monster's behalf.

Carl Van Doren has written that *The Stray Lamb* was "little noted in a year resounding with Hemingway's *A Farewell to Arms*, Evelyn Scott's *The Wave*, William Faulkner's *The Sound and the Fury*, Thomas Wolfe's *Look Homeward Angel*."[55] But these are, in all reality, novels in a different class than *The Stray Lamb*. While an argument might be, and has been made, that *The Stray Lamb* is a novel of redemption and of salvation, a serious literary work posing as comedy, the novel is nothing more than an "entertainment." The truth is that the 1920s could not have ended better for Thorne Smith than with *The Stray Lamb*. It proved that *Topper* was no fluke, and that the writer had a distinctive and original comedic style.

1. Roland Young and Thorne Smith among Others, Thorne Smith: His Life and Times, p. 8.

2. Ibid, p. 8.

3. Ibid, pp. 15-16.

4. Joseph Leo Blotner, Thorne Smith: A Study in Popular Fiction, p. 11.

5. Malcolm Cowley, ed., Writers at Work: The Paris Review Interviews, p. 72.

6. Quoted in Michael D. Walker, "Host to Said Ghosts: The Thorne Smith Story," p. 41.

7. Stephen Whitlock, "A Fanciful, Haunting Tale of Influence," p. 18.

8. Lewis E. Frank to Joseph Leo Blotner, quoted in Thorne Smith: A Study in Popular Fiction, p. 12.

9. Biltmore Oswald: The Diary of a Hapless Recruit, p. 1

10. Ibid, p. 3

11. Ibid, p. 39.

12. Ibid, p. 41.

13. Out o' Luck: Biltmore Oswald Very Much at Sea, p. 48.

14. Ibid, p. 67.

15. Ibid, p. 71 and elsewhere.

16. Ibid, p. 103.

17. Biltmore Oswald: The Diary of a Hapless Recruit, p. 53.

18. Ibid, p. 87.

19. Roland Young and Thorne Smith among Others, Thorne Smith: His Life and Times, p. 6.

20. Joseph Leo Blotner, Thorne Smith: A Study in Popular Fiction, p. 87.

21. Topper, p. 218.

22. Roland Young and Thorne Smith among Others, Thorne Smith: His Life and Times, p. 27.

23. The Stray Lamb, p. 141.

24. Roland Young and Thorne Smith among Others, Thorne Smith: His Life and Times, p. 24.

25. Topper, p. 6.

26. Ibid, p. 96.

27. Ibid, p. 120.

28. Ibid, p. 25.

29. Dial, vol. LXVII, 1919, p. 358.

30. Civilization in the United States, p. iii.

31. Harold Stearns, The Confessions of a Harvard Man: The Street I Know, p. 193.

32. Ibid, pp. 384-385.

33. Ibid, p. 388.

34. Ibid, p. 391.

35. Ibid, p. 385.

36. Ibid, p. 377.

37. Marion died on October 13, 2000.

38. Joseph Blotner to Anthony Slide, September 1, 2009.

39. Dream's End, p. 22.

40. Ibid, p. 22.

41. H. Allen Smith, People Named Smith, p. 179.

42. James Thurber, The Years with Ross, pp. 146-147.

43. Dream's End, p. 20.

44. Ibid, p. 166.

45. Roland Young and Thorne Smith among Others, Thorne Smith: His Life and Times, p. 27.

46. "Gossip of the Book World," Los Angeles Times, July 1, 1934, p. A6.

47. Roland Young and Thorne Smith among Others, Thorne Smith: His Life and Times, p. 28.

48. Information taken from Joseph Leo Blotner, Thorne Smith: A Study in Popular Fiction, pp. 27-28.

49. Michael D. Walker, "Host to Said Ghosts: The Thorne Smith Story," p. 43.

50. Stephen Goldin, "The Stray Lamb," p. 1850.

51. Edwin Schallert, "'Stray Lamb' Reckoned Good for Hope or Grant," Los Angeles Times, August 12, 1944, p. 5.

52. "If Bill Cagney talks Frank Capra into making Thorne Smith's The Stray Lamb I'll be surprised," wrote Hedda Hopper in her July 18, 1945 gossip column. She remained unsurprised.

53. See Patrick McGilligan, Cagney: The Actor as Auteur, p. 182, and the New York Times, March 6, 1955.

54. Michael D. Walker, "Host to Said Ghosts: The Thorne Smith Story," p. 43.

55. Carl Van Doren, The American Novel, 1789-1939, p. 325.

CHAPTER TWO

TOPPER

The 1926 publication of *Topper*, followed by the 1929 publication of
a serious work, *Dream's End*, meant an end to Smith's employment as a
copy writer and the beginning of a full-time career as a novelist. *Topper*
represents the cornerstone of its writer's reputation. It is his best known
novel. It, along with a 1932 sequel, *Topper Takes a Trip*, formed the basis
for three motion picture films. Above all, Thorne Smith created a formula
with *Topper* that he was to follow for all the comic novels that came later.
The pattern and the "farce technique," as Joseph Blotner calls it, remained
basically the same. As Blotner notes,

"The basic ingredients of the formula include the supernatural, sex, liquor,
and satire. The main themes are the marital unhappiness of the hero, who
is usually a well-to-do executive, woman the pursuer, in the person of the
Hero's feminine companion, and the complete change of the hero's basic
values, attitudes and behavior. The season is almost invariably summer,
while the action most often takes place in New York City and residential
suburbs peopled by commuters, though it sometimes shifts to the seashore.
He also makes frequent use of department stores, hotels, swimming pools
and Turkish baths as settings for incidents, and there is often a commut-
ing scene on a train or subway. Servants, usually old family retainers, are
invariably the confidants of the main characters, and animals always appear,
in most cases as pets of the heroes. Almost all the novels also include the
arrest of the principals by police and a court scene which follows."[1]

DID SHE FALL?

However, the novelist seemed still uncertain as to whether his future
clearly lay in comedy or whether he needed to prove to himself and his
readership that he was adept at other genres. Unfortunately, he really was

not, but that did not prevent Thorne Smith's publishing in 1930 a mystery novel that was obviously influenced by Dashiell Hammett. The subject of the question *Did She Fall?* is Emily-Jane Seabrook, an unscrupulous young lady who ingratiates herself into the lives of her male friends and plans to marry Barney Crewe, because he fills her requirements of "dumb, rich and idealistic."[2] After a confrontation with Barney's brother Daniel and Lane Holt, a young man with whom she is in a current relationship, Emily-Jane falls to her death from a cliff top. Scott Munson is put in charge of the case by the district attorney, and his investigation reveals that Emily-Jane was wrenched off the cliff top by Daniel's fiancée June Lansing, standing on a ledge and pulling the other woman's ankle. Scott is "aided" in his investigation by two comic police officers, both named Tim Shay, and both singularly irritating and unfunny.

A friend of Daniel, Dr. Manning, helps him and June to escape on his son's yacht. Faithful servants lie to protect June, and Scott is easily persuaded to drop the case. Ultimately, Scott's loyalty lies with high society rather than the law. A year later, Daniel and June meet up with Manning, Barney and a new girlfriend in Switzerland. There, they receive an affectionate note from Scott, inviting them to join him for the winter in Egypt. Scott Munson's behavior is justified by Thorne Smith in the opening sentences of the novel:

"Sometimes a well-executed murder clears the air. This observation is in no sense suggestively advanced. But the fact is that in virtually all groups, communities, and gatherings of human beings there are certain members who would be far, far better out of the way…persons whose speedy absence would result in more actual good that would their continued presence."[3]

Did She Fall? is, by turns, melodramatic and engrossing. The text, however, seems hurried and, at times, poorly constructed. Where is the editing to sort out such discrepancies as on page 181, when we read "all that night in Daniel's room the light was kept burning," followed by the next sentence beginning, "Whenever he turned it out."

The novel, dedicated to the parents of Smith's wife, was to sell almost a million copies. It was reprinted by Doubleday, Doran in August 1932, and had gone through three printings by July 1935; two years later, *Did She Fall?* was published in a cheap Sun Dial Press edition, and went through six printings before the Pocket Books paperback edition came out in December 1947. Yet, and quite rightly, contemporary critical response was restrained. While the reviewer for the *New York World* (August 17, 1930) described it as "undoubtedly a first-rate novelty in the way of a mystery tale," no less a personage than Dashiell Hammett wrote in the *New York Evening Post* (September 6, 1930), "At times the book approaches something akin to literature but over-writing, rickety construction, triteness of invention and a flabby sort of whimsicality make it in the end only an indifferent detective story."

It is perhaps ironic that Dashiell Hammett may possibly have borrowed from Thorne Smith's creations in *Topper*, Marion and George Kerby, and remade them as Nick and Nora Charles in *The Thin Man*, published in serial form in *Redbook* magazine in 1933 and as a novel the following year. There is certainly some similarity in terms of the repartee between Nick and Nora Charles and the Kerbys, although the wit and speed of the dialogue in the subsequent "Thin Man" film series probably owes more to screenwriters Albert Hackett and Frances Goodrich than to Dashiell Hammett.

Many years later, in a perceptive analysis of the book in *Armchair Detective*, Gary Hoppenstand wrote, "If F. Scott Fitzgerald had written a detective novel, it might have resembled Thorne Smith's *Did She Fall?* Like Fitzgerald, Smith truly evokes the period in which he wrote. And though *Did She Fall?* was published in 1930 near the start of America's Great Depression, it is more reflective of Jay Gatsby's world — the 1920s era of flappers and rebellious youths and liberated sexuality and perceived moral isolation. Smith attempts to show the reader the effects that a vicious social climber has upon a moneyed, upper-crust and socially remote family, a family that is perhaps as reprehensible as the social climber. The murder mystery for Smith, it turns out, is merely a device in which it is revealed the evils of 'high society,' much as Fitzgerald does in *The Great Gatsby*."[4]

In all probability, it is *Topper* that persuaded readers to purchase *Did She Fall?* It is *Topper* against which those readers judged the new book — and found it wanting. That Smith considered the need to add comic policemen to his new novel is indicative of just how obvious it had become to him what his public expected, no matter what he might have wanted to deliver.

TOPPER

According to Smith, *Topper: An Improbable Adventure* (to give the novel its full title) began life as a short story. "My wife needed clothes so that she could appear covered if not clad in public. After I had done the first ten pages I suddenly realized I had written a swell first chapter for a book. I told this to my wife. She sighed and went back to bed. Some months later I bought her a frock of sorts and she sallied forth to see what changes had taken place in the city during her enforced absence from it."[5]

Thorne Smith plotted *Topper* while on vacation in Bermuda in September 1924. He wrote a first draft immediately upon his return to New York.

Not surprisingly, Smith dedicates *Topper* to Celia, "to say the least." The novel recounts the story of Cosmo Topper, a banking executive, "nearly forty and acquiring flesh"[6] who "could excuse nature and the Republican Party, but not man,"[7] and who lives with his wife (with no first name) and a cat Scollops in suburban middle-class boredom and misery. She tells him what is for dinner, "You like lamb," and he lacks the courage to respond that he is "not particularly lustful for lamb."[8]

Topper's redemption from middle-class malaise comes about thanks to a wealthy pair, George and Marion Kerby, "the fastest young couple in town,"[9] who were killed in an automobile crash. Topper is highly attracted to the car involved in the crash, which he acquires from Mark, a local garage owner, along with, as it transpires, the ghosts of the young couple. As Marion Kerby later explains, "We are what you might call low-planed spirits…We are authentic spirits"[10] with access to a certain amount of ectoplasm. She will sing of the accident to Topper,

I once was a lady as you may divine.
Though the fact it is hard for to see.
Rare beauty and riches and romance were mine,
Before I ran into a tree.
My husband he did it. The devil would drive,
The high-flying, low-lying soak.
And that is the reason I'm no more alive,
For he ran me smack into an oak.

Chapter Four reveals, "Mr. Topper's secret life dated from the Saturday on which he purchased the Kerbys' ill-fated car from Mark."[11] The latter teaches Topper to drive; the car is introduced to Mrs. Topper, who is not pleased, particularly as it and her husband's late appearance means the leg of lamb has spoiled. "Damn the leg of lamb!"[12] exclaims a newly revitalized Topper.

As Topper drives his new purchase, he passes the tree into which the Kerbys had crashed the car, and, moments later, the couple themselves have joined him in the car, unseen, but definitely there, with Topper seated in Marion Kerby's lap. Later, Topper drives his wife into town, only to discover that she has purchased a car for herself, a car that he has accidentally driven into while parking. Not surprisingly, Topper decides to return to the tree where he had last been with the Kerbys. "George and Marion Kerby were vastly more acceptable to him than the people who constituted his social circle."[13]

With George conveniently disappearing for a while — and half the novel — Topper and Marion Kerby embark on a series of adventures. They arrive at a Connecticut Hotel and meet up with two other ghosts, Colonel Arthur Scott and his mistress Mrs. Hart, who are accompanied by their phantom dog Oscar. (Like Mrs. Topper, Mrs. Hart has no last name; and because she is first introduced as Mrs. Scott, many commentators have incorrectly identified her as the Colonel's wife.) The relationship between Topper and Marion Kerby is never fully written out, although they do share a bed together. If sexual intercourse is involved, it is not delineated, neither is the matter of how Topper might enjoy sex with a ghost. Marion has no problem with her relationship with Topper in that, as she points out, marriage vows are only until death do us part. Eventually, the group, along with a returned George Kerby, take to the road — and there is another crash. Topper has one last kiss with Marion Kerby, who tells him, "I'm moving on...Some day we'll meet again, perhaps but things will be different there."[14]

Topper's farewell to Marion Kerby captures the feelings that many a lonely or lost man must have felt at the end of his one, true, but unlasting relationship:

"You created happiness in me...You've awakened dreams and left memories. You've made me humble and you've made me human. You've taught me to understand how a man with a hangover feels. You've lifted me forever out of the rut of my smug existence. I'll go back to it I know, but I won't be the same man."[15]

When Topper returns to consciousness, he is in the hospital being visited by Mrs. Topper. She has changed somewhat. Not only has she tried on the step-ins that Topper had acquired for her early in the story, but she had found them lovely and acquired a lot more. As Topper falls asleep, he dreams of Marion Kerby drifting further and further away from him, and of introducing Scollops to Oscar, with the latter amusing the cat for hours by making his head and tail alternately disappear.

The comment of the critic in the *New York Evening Post* typifies the reaction of readers at the time and in years to come: "Your eyes are filled with tears from laughter over its wild absurdities."[16] Unfortunately, *Topper* seems to have received little attention from major publications at its initial publication. A small-town newspaper in Illinois, *Forest Park Review* (May 14, 1926) did critique and did like the novel, commenting at the conclusion of the piece, "In Mr. Topper Mr. Smith has created a character, appealing because he is human and pitiful and ridiculous who is worthy of extended life." An anonymous librarian at the Los Angeles Central Library reviewed the novel for possible acquisition, describing its literary merit as "fair" and its permanent value as "none." He or she continued, "The ridiculous situations caused by the materialization and their sudden disappearance of these spirit friends are so cleverly drawn that the book is a big laugh all the way."

As one reads the *Topper* books, one is reminded that there are elements of that uniquely American, uniquely motion picture-related and uniquely 1930s genre, the screwball comedy, to be found here. Thorne Smith's leading men (at least the good-looking ones) often stir up images of Cary Grant, while his leading ladies remind one of Carole Lombard. The latter never appeared in a Thorne Smith screen adaptation, but Cary Grant did agree to appear as George Kerby in the film version of *Topper*.

As early as 1933, the *Los Angeles Times* had hoped that *Topper* might reach the screen — "cleaned up a bit"[17] — but there was to be a three-year hiatus before the screen rights were acquired by Hal Roach Studios, Inc. for $10,000.00. It is possible that Universal had an option on the screen rights at the same time the company purchased *The Night Life of the Gods*. Hal Roach (1892-1992) was one of America's leading comedy producers, responsible for the early films of Harold Lloyd and for the teaming of Stan Laurel and Oliver Hardy. Prior to the production of *Topper*, Roach had made only a limited number of feature films, with those primarily starring Laurel and Hardy. *Topper*, released by Metro-Goldwyn-Mayer, had a reported budget of $500,000.00, and is often described at the time as his first "A" feature, although such a label might be applied to the Laurel and Hardy vehicles. The "A" feature designation was, of course, in large part due to the film's top star, Cary Grant, although he had yet to make the greatest of his screwball comedies, *The Awful Truth*, *Bringing up Baby* and *Holiday*. As Hal Roach recalled in an interview with Elizabeth Ward,

"At that time, Cary Grant was a friend of mine. He had rented a house in Santa Monica with Randolph Scott, next door to my very good friend

Townsend 'Tee' Netcher [a business man]. Netcher's place was only fifteen minutes away from my Culver City studio, and in the summertime I used to go down to lunch and swim with them practically every day. Scott and Grant were usually there, too. So when I read *Topper* I thought of Cary for the part and talked it over with him, and he decided to do the picture."[18]

Three writers were assigned to the project: Eddie Moran, Jack Jevne, who had written for Laurel and Hardy, and Eric Hatch, who was responsible for the novel, *My Man Godfrey*, revising an earlier script written by Jeannie Macpherson, who is usually associated with the films of Cecil B. DeMille. Just as the writers omit Colonel Scott and Mrs Hart, obviously because of their relationship, also left out of the screen adaptation is Oscar the dog. However, the writers do somewhat make up for this oversight by including a quizzical dog who watches with two yokels as ghostly George Kerby changes a tire, and, later, by displaying an advert for a dog show at the Seabreeze Hotel and having two large dogs on prominent display there, one of which is supposedly thrown through the air by the Kerbys (obviously with the use of wires).

Norman Z. McLeod was hired to direct at $2,500.00 per week for a ten week production schedule. Not surprisingly, Cary Grant, as George Kerby, was the top paid actor, receiving $75,000.00 for twenty-six days work. Constance Bennett, as Marion Kerby, received $40,000.00 for thirty day work, Roland Young in the title role received $15,000.00 for thirty-three days work, while Billie Burke, as Mrs. Topper, received $8,000.00 for seven days work.[19]

There are unconfirmed reports that W.C. Fields was at one time considered for the title role. Apparently, if he was offered the role, he turned it down, and, happily, the producer decided to offer the part to Roland Young.

ROLAND YOUNG

It seems both natural and appropriate that Thorne Smith's friend Roland Young should have been cast as Cosmo Topper. If ever an actor was born to play the role it was Young. As Carolyn See has written, Smith's "heroes are as lonely as the loneliest children,"[20] and there is no actor who has such a sense of being a solitary individual, isolated almost but quite happy in his own world as Roland Young. Smith and the actor had been close since 1930. A year later, Smith wrote a play for his friend, in which Young was to portray a gentleman who inherits an estate complete with three mistresses. Nothing came of that project, and the manuscript is no longer extant. Thorne Smith inscribed a copy of *Topper* to the actor, describing him as "The Most disarming 'gentleman Johnnie' that ever advanced the lines of G.B.S."[21] The George Bernard Shaw

Thorne Smith's favorite actor, Roland Young.

reference is presumably to Young's performance as General Burgoyne in the London production of *The Devil's Disciple* in 1923.

Smith's daughters remembered Young as a frequent visitor to the family home. He would come over and eat cheese and drink beer with their father.[22]

Roland Young begins to comprehend just what Cary Grant and Constance Bennett have in store for him in Topper.

Roland Young's name appears as the lead author of a thirty-two page monograph, *Thorne Smith: His Life and Times with a Note on His Books & A Complete Bibliography*, published by Doubleday, Doran in 1934. The paperback volume contains a sketch of Smith by Young, along with an amusing interview, during which the pair imbibes freely and calls themselves "Mr. Smith" and "Mr. Young." It is an amusing, if not particularly informative, piece.[23]

Born in London on November 11, 1887, Roland Young had made his stage debut there in 1908. He came to New York four years later, becoming an American citizen in 1918. As *Time* magazine (June 15, 1953) wrote at the time of his death in New York on June 5, 1953, his "clipped moustache, clipped accent and acidly debonair style made him a comic stand-by of the U.S. screen for more than two decades." Roland Young had been busy in films since 1929, with his best known performances being in *His Double Life*, *Ruggles of Red Gap*, *David Copperfield*, *The Philadelphia Story*, and *The Man Who Could Work Miracles*. It was, however, as Topper, that he is best remembered; indeed the *Los Angeles Times* (June 7, 1953) headed a report of his death with the words "best known for roles in 'Topper' pictures." Young was not only seen as Topper in three Hal Roach films, but also heard on NBC radio as Topper. *The Adventures of Topper* was first heard on NBC on June 7, 1945, as a summer series sponsored by Post Toasties, with Paul Mann and Frances Chaney as the Kerbys and Hope Emerson as Mrs. Topper.

In his unpublished autobiography, the actor makes it very clear that he prefered the stage to the film:

"When you rehearse in a play and play it, you begin at the beginning of Act I, go all through Act I, Act II, and Act III, whereas in a picture, by reason of the manner in which they have to be made for economic reasons, you may start in the middle, or towards the end, and go back and forth until you have made the whole picture, but you never have any sense of a logical sequence. In addition to this, there is the fact that while you are playing a part in a picture, the whole stage has to be deathly quiet, whereas when you are playing a part on the stage, you have the instant, if any, response of the audience. You don't make so much money on the stage, but you have a great deal more fun. Also, you live at least a part of the time in New York which, after all, is a city, whereas Hollywood is a suburb of a suburb."

Young's other objection to films is dubious in that it questions the very reason why he is so brilliant in the *Topper* films: "Pretty soon after I had started in Hollywood I became typed, and with a few welcome excursions into more notable efforts, I played milquetoast characters pretty consistently. Why is it that I enjoy dramatic parts rather than comedy I am not quite sure, because comedy is a very grateful medium, but I look back very fondly to essentially dramatic characters like Neil McCrae in *Beggar on Horseback*."[24]

Roland Young generally gave interviews with a martini glass in his hand, gravely contemplating the necessary ingredients laid out in front of him. As he explained to the *New York Times* (January 20, 1935), his directors were "very nice fellows, really. But it's the system you know. A red script, a blue script, a buff script, a yellow script, finally a white script. Then they throw away the white script. Terrible, really."

To a large extent, Roland Young would be typecast as Topper. So much so, that he recalled waiting to cross New York's Park Avenue, outside the U.S.O. during World War Two and suddenly having a young sailor take his arm, saying, "I'll see you across the street, Mr. Topper." Young's response was typical: "This act of kindness made me feel exactly one hun-

As George and Marion Kerby, Cary Grant and Constance Bennett materialize in Topper.

dred and six years old. 'Do,' I often ask myself, 'good Samaritans effect more good than harm or vice versa?'"[25]

One thing that the Hal Roach Studios did not need to worry about was Topper's attire. Roland Young provided his own business suits.

The special effects in the film were the work of thirty-two-year-old Roy Seawright, who had worked for Hal Roach since the age of fifteen. He was asked to create a series of effects while the producer had the novel under option, and once the effects proved satisfactory, Roach went ahead and acquired the rights. As Seawright explained to the *Los Angeles Times*, most of his effects, including split screen, matte shots, animation, and double exposure, were actually outgrowths from the two-reel comedy days of the silent era.[26] The best special effects sequence is undoubtedly that showing an invisible George Kerby changing a tire. Roy Seawright did not receive an Academy Award nomination for his work on *Topper*, but he was nominated for Best Special Effects for the other two productions, *Topper Takes a Trip* and *Topper Returns*.

Watching *Topper* today in the newly preserved version from the UCLA Film and Television Archive, one is perhaps aware that the images are slightly fuzzy. The film was in fact photographed in somewhat blurry fashion. It seems that cinematographer Norbert Brodine deliberately used diffusion in order to hide the wires used to move the props in a number of scenes. For consistency, he decided to use this same soft, slightly blurry, diffused "look" not just for the special effects shots but for every scene in the film.

Initially, the Production Code Administration was enthusiastic of the project, with Joseph Breen writing to Roach's Mat O'Brien on June 1, 1936 that, "It is our opinion that this story has good entertainment values, and that it can be made into a motion picture which will be acceptable from the standpoint of the Production Code."[27] However, by March 18, 1937, Breen was telling O'Brien that the "story is in violation of the principles of the Production Code." There were problems with the "sexual implication" of Marion Kerby's efforts to rejuvenate Topper, which were sorted out the following day in conference. Equally problematical was the business with the "pants" (the step-ins) flying through the air, being grabbed by Topper and their discovery by Mrs. Topper. "There will be no reference to them as 'pants' throughout the picture," Breen informed the studio. It was agreed that the reaction of a fat lady to being hit on the posterior should remain, but not her line, "I'm not accustomed to being slapped in the lobby."

Based on a design by Anthony Garrity, LaMar Bresee of Pasadena was responsible for building the sports roadster body, mounted on a Buick chassis, so important to the storyline. The film began shooting, without incident, on March 25, 1937, and was completed by late May of the same year.

Topper also marks the screen debut of composer Hoagy Carmichael, who wrote the song "Old Man Moon" for the film, and performed it along with Constance Bennett and Cary Grant. In the first reel of the film, as George and Marion Kerby spend an evening moving from one nightclub to the next, with the change of locale shown through a change in orchestra, they end up in a small bar, whose owner is anxious to close, and whose pianist is Carmichael. The transition from one nightspot to another is handled with admirable skill and direction, and, in a way, nothing could be more perfect than its ending with Hoagy Carmichael.

Topper is unquestionably the best of the Thorne Smith screen adaptations, and is basically faithful to the novel at least in general terms. The major change is that the Kerbys are very much alive for almost the first third of the film, helping to provide the audience with an idea of the type of behavior to which they were prone, and also the cheerful manner

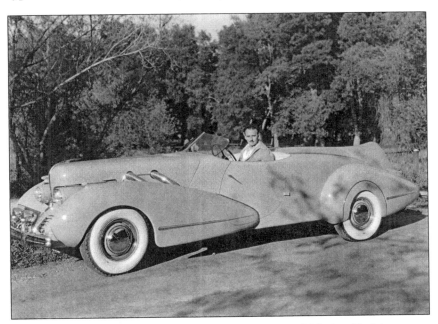

Topper *director Norman Z. McLeod seated in George and Marion Kerby's car.*

in which they upset Topper's moral stance. In order to provide for the Kerbys and Topper knowing each other, the film has George Kerby as a major shareholder in Topper's bank. Topper is also promoted in the screen adaptation from bank manager to bank president. (A film with a banker as a sympathetic character must seem something of an anachronism to a 21st century audience.)

Cary Grant and Constance Bennett are the film's stars, although, as with the novel, Cary Grant as George Kerby is missing for a lengthy section towards the end. Neither Roland Young nor Billie Burke resembles Mr. and Mrs. Topper as depicted by Thorne Smith, but their casting could not have been closer to perfection.[28] Similarly, while Topper has no butler in the novel, the addition of one, as played by Alan Mowbray, is a stroke of genius.

Topper the film boasts some great character performances, not only by Young, Burke and Mowbray, but also by Virginia Sale as Topper's secretary Miss Johnson, who attempts to brighten up her rather dour appearance after discovering that her boss is somewhat of a playboy. Equally adept at lighting up the screen with their presence are Eugene Pallette as a

Topper: *Alan Mowbray, as Wilkins the butler, expresses his displeasure at the first meeting between Billie Burke, as Mrs. Topper, and Cary Grant, as George Kerby.*

much-put-upon house detective at the Seabreeze Hotel[29] where Topper has checked in, Hedda Hopper as Mrs. Stuyvesant, a socialite neighbor of the Toppers who takes an interest in the household once Topper has been exposed as drunk and disorderly, and Arthur Lake as an elevator boy at the Kerbys' New York apartment who later re-encounters Topper and company at the Seabreeze Hotel, where he has sought new employment.

Jaunty music over the main titles, courtesy of Roach in-house composer Marvin Hatley[30] gives good promise of a jaunty film that is to follow — and the promise is almost kept. Certainly, *Topper* boasts a great cast, good direction and strong production values. At the same time, there are one or two slow sequences, and the film could have been tightened somewhat.

Topper makes his appearance in reel two, some ten minutes into the film, taking his morning shower. That is about the only freedom that the poor man enjoys, as butler Alan Mowbray controls the bathrobe he is to put on, while Mrs. Topper has organized his entire schedule, even down to the exact moment he must leave for the office and what his breakfast

George and Marion Kerby (Cary Grant and Constance Bennett) encounter detective Casey (Eugene Pallette) at the Seabreeze Hotel in Topper.

will consist of. There is even a reference to lamb for dinner.

As the story progresses, Roland Young never loses his domination of the film, despite the antics of Grant and Bennett. There is something magical about the little dance he does in his office after an encounter with Marion Kerby. There is something almost lyrical to the scene where he picks up the handkerchief that she has dropped, sniffs it and comments, "I wonder why Marion Kerby reminds me of an angel." In the next sequence, Marion Kerby will be dead — but anything other than an angel.

Billie Burke is probably one of the most talented of comedic charac-ter actresses, and she has never been better than here. After Topper has been injured in a car crash, he comes back to life in bed. At his side is

Billie Burke who quietly lifts her skirt to show him that she is wearing the lace underwear that had earlier so outraged her. It is a magnificently gentle yet humorous moment which works because the audience cannot see what she is wearing, or ever that her dress is raised, but all is evident from Roland Young's fascinated stare and Billie Burke's soft smile.

The tender, comic moment between Roland Young and Billie Burke, as Mr. and Mrs. Topper, with which Topper *concludes.*

In 1985, *Topper* made film history as the first film to be colorized — by Hal Roach Film Studios, Inc. and Colorization, Inc. Happily, the original version is pure black-and-white, with the only "color" to be found in the drama relating to those lace underpants.

While *Topper* the film as much as *Topper* the novel may have influenced later film and television productions, the motion picture is not the first to feature a very busy ghost. *Berkeley Square* (1933), based on Henry James, has a ghost of the past involved with his namesake of the present, both played by Leslie Howard. In *The Scoundrel* (1935), Noel Coward is an intellectually superior but most unloved one. Robert Donat is a lively Scottish ghost in *The Ghost Goes West* (1936), which is in many respects, aside from the historic background of the story, closest to *Topper*.

Some modern critics have noted that unlike screwball comedies of the period, such as *My Man Godfrey* and *Sullivan's Travels*, *Topper* does not acknowledge a class system in the United States. The hero of *Topper* the film is a bank president, depicted, quite extraordinarily if one considers it, as a victim of the system. The freedom that he attains is the result of his being as wealthy and becoming as childish in many ways as the Kerbys. Much similar criticism might also be directed at the novel, except that there Topper is not a bank president and the Kerbys are never presented as inordinately wealthy.

Upon Topper's release in July 1937, critical response was mixed. *Variety* (July 14, 1937) worried that "The rank and file of theatergoers will experience difficulty in following strange and surprising twists of the story, and are not likely to distinguish easily the passages of realism from the sequence of unreality." Further, the reviewer did not appear to be as familiar with the works of Thorne Smith and their popularity as one might expect. "Effort to excuse the absurdities on the theory that the intent is farce comedy does not entirely excuse the production from severe rebuke," he wrote. "Fact also that the living dead always are facetious may be shocking to sensibilities. Some of the situations and dialog offend conventional good taste." In *The New Yorker* (August 28, 1937), John Mosher hailed it as a "summer giggle." Eileen Creelman in the *New York Sun* (August 20, 1937) predicted that *Topper* "should start a wave of laughter." *Life* magazine (July 26, 1937) picked *Topper* as "Movie of the Week," noting that director Norman Z. McLeod, who had worked as an animator during the silent era, would often make pencil sketches in an effort to have his actors understand what he was hoping to accomplish. The magazine also published some of the sketches side by side with scenes from the film to illustrate how well the technique worked. McLeod's direction of the film is unassuming, never emphatic or intrusive. And while it is easy to ignore the director's contribution, it is McLeod to whom modern audiences should be grateful for his handling of the comedy material. Just as *Topper* benefits from McLeod's presence, so do many other comedy films, such as the Marx Brothers vehicles *Monkey Business* and *Horse Feathers*, W.C. Fields' *It's a Gift* (1934), Danny Kaye's *The Secret Life of Walter Mitty* (1947), and Bob Hope's *The Paleface* (1948).

Newsweek (August 7, 1937) was as positive as *Life* about the film: "Expertly produced by Hal Roach and spiced with some of the cleverest camera tricks to date, this adaptation of the late Thorne Smith's novel achieves bright and airy comedy with none of the gruesome overtones inherent in the subject matter." The most damning review was published in the *New York Times* (August 20, 1937), whose critic wrote:

"Thorne Smith's yarn...possessed all the delicious whimsy which in the film is only a mechanically garnished dish of whimsy substitute. We honestly regret our inability to shout hurray for *Topper*, because everybody seems to have tried hard to make it click...Whimsy is a delicate and perishable commodity and nobody need be blamed for the slight spoilage in transit...Mr. Young and his fellow players are responsible for whatever success an otherwise completely irresponsible film enjoys."

Topper opened in Los Angeles at Grauman's Chinese Theatre on August 11, 1937. It was not considered strong enough to stand on its own, and played on a double bill with *Between Two Women*, starring Franchot Tone and Maureen O'Sullivan. As a promotional gimmick, two Constance Bennett and Cary Grant look-a-likes were sent out around Hollywood in a limousine. "*Topper*...is full of tricks," wrote Philip K. Scheuer in the *Los Angeles Times* (July 18, 1937). "Some of the tricks are wonderful to behold; but like all trick films, this one has no heart, and it takes an unconscionably long while to get going. Roland Young...saves it — he and the cameraman." Scheuer returned to the film on August 12, 1937, with somewhat more enthusiastm, noting, "it is bubbling over with disappearing acts, ectoplasmic manifestations and the like."

Women's clubs were surprisingly supportive of the production, although the Daughters of the American Revolution felt it necessary to point out that "social leaders do not rush to the homes of suddenly-notorious strangers." The West Coast branch of the General Federation of Women's Clubs warned of "excessive drinking," while the National Society of New England Women also cautioned that "Both ghosts and mortals imbibe rather freely."

Rightfully, Roland Young was nominated for an Academy Award for Best Supporting Actor for his work in the film. For its contribution, the Hal Roach Studio Sound Department, Elmer A. Raguse, Sound Director, also received a nomination for Best Sound Recording. The Department also received a nomination for its work on *Topper Returns*.

TOPPER TAKES A TRIP

Thorne Smith may well be said to have used his time on the French Riviera in 1928 to research *Topper Takes a Trip*. In the original manuscript, but subsequently deleted, he wrote about blasé American expatriates in France. It may certainly be that the villa in Nice which Topper has rented is similar to that occupied by Smith and his family. He was experiencing melancholy not only at an inability to put pen to paper but also at the remembrance of life in France. Both he and his wife had begun serious drinking, and the lack of funds for bootleg alcohol was driving the novelist to desperation. According to Joseph Blotner, Smith wrote love poetry for a young man unable to produce anything suitable for his girlfriend. In return, the young man provided the novelist with something called "brown gin."[31]

"I like the book," Smith wrote Roland Young. "It's quite disgusting."[32] Later, he wrote the actor, asking permission to dedicate the new novel to him, and when such permission was granted, the writer responded,

"Your name goes into the book without flourishes, and I have a feeling, old top, that it's going to bring me luck.

"Thank God I have recovered some of my customary urbanity. No one can be sadder than a sad Irishman and a disgruntled humorist. As a matter of fact most all the time I have a carefully suppressed strata of discontent. Most persons have, I think. I live near the river, and every time I hear a liner blow the whistle for departure I writhe inwardly."[33]

Topper Takes a Trip was published in May 1932, with a simple inscription, "For Roland Young."

The novel opens with Topper in blue silk pajamas contemplating the Mediterranean, while the Mediterranean looks back at him. "Kindred spirits well met, contemplating each other across an alluring girdle of sand."[34] The sand is made even more alluring by the daily presence of a sun-bathing German model and ongoing thoughts as to how much she might reveal today. In an effort to furbish his relations with his wife, Topper had taken her to France, along with Scollops the cat. Sadly, little has changed in the relationship, with Mrs. Topper now planning "gigot" for lunch.

Unfortunately or perhaps fortuitously for Topper, also in France are the Kerbys, Colonel Scott, Mrs. Hart and Oscar the dog. Topper first encounters George Kerby in the bathtub, hot water for which is provided by a heater nicknamed Vesuvius. All at once, things return to chaotic normality as the group visit the beach, the racetrack, a hotel, the casino in Monaco,[35] and, of course, a courtroom. It is all very formulaic, very episodic, and almost a repeat of what takes place in the original novel. George

Kerby goes off with a lady friend for a couple of weeks and Topper and Marion Kerby are once again thrown together, spending several nights in the same bedroom and the same bed. If there was any question about the relationship between the two in *Topper*, the sequel confirms that it was consummated. Of course, as with all Smith's novels, the sex is never explicit or detailed in any fashion. Various ladies, including the German model, are disrobed in pursuit of humor, and a few gentlemen are stripped down to their drawers. Even Mrs. Topper loses her night attire at one point and is viewed nude by George Kerby. "I assure you you need have no fear for the honor of Mrs. Topper," Kerby tells Topper.[36]

Ultimately, determined not to lose Topper, Marion Kerby considers having him join her and the rest of the company. "Women have killed men to keep other women from having them, but here was a woman attempting to murder her lover in order to keep him with her."[37] Topper declares himself "An American Tragedy."Taking a large gun, Marion considers the options as to where to aim. Unfortunately, when she does fire the weapon, Topper is only wounded, and in the buttocks. When George tells Marion that the Colonel will fix him up as good as new, Marion sobs, "That's just the trouble...I don't want him as good as new. I want him all dead."[38] Rather as he did in the first novel, Topper acknowledges that Marion is no longer with him and that without her he is no longer the same man:

"Topper did not philosophize over the absence of Marion. He was hurt as an animal is hurt, and like an animal he remained dumb. He did not tell himself in so many words that with the vanishing of Marion also vanished much of himself — that she had carried away with her the glamour and buoyancy of life, its mirthfulness and romance. Inside him this knowledge was making itself poignantly felt. Topper did not try to analyze it. Topper was not that way."[39]

At the close, Marion is gone, Mrs. Topper is speeding towards her husband, and he is alone save for Scollops. "He fears very much that he will always be alone."[40] He does have the scar to remind him of Marion, and there was always Félice, the French maid. "Topper turned to the French windows behind which Félice was waiting. She was not. Félice was sound asleep. However..."[41]

Topper Takes a Trip ends on a poignant note. The French visit is coming to an end and Topper sadly considers the life to which he is about to return. How many vacationers have had similar thoughts, depressed at a return to the same routine, to the same boredom, the same futility of existence. Topper's thoughts must very much have echoed those of his creator, who was never happier than in France. Throughout, one is much aware of Smith's empathy for the French people, for French customs and for the French lifestyle.

Banker Topper finds himself in a French jail, confronting jailer Eddie Conrad, in Topper Takes a Trip.

The novel does provide a couple of answers to unspoken questions arising from the original work. Mrs. Topper's first name is revealed as Mary, despite the three film versions referring to her as Clara. In *Topper*, the couple lived on Glendale Avenue. Here it is revealed that the township in which they reside is also called Glendale. Some readers might be confused and assume this is Glendale, California, but nowhere does Thorne Smith suggest anything of the sort. The first novel was set on the East Coast, and the Toppers have not moved West since it was written.

Initial sales were disappointing — just a little over 10,000 — but ultimately *Topper Takes a Trip* sold over a million in less than two decades.

Perhaps readers were put off by the lack of enthusiasm from the critics? The *Saturday Review of Literature* (May 21, 1932), for example, commented,

"There are many merry, mad scenes, and plenty of good clean dirt. But to the admirers of Mr. Smith this may nevertheless be a slight disappointment. There is nothing in the present book that is altogether equal to the court-room scene in *Turnabout*, or the hero's conversation with his books. But although, like his spooks, Mr. Smith may have temporarily abandoned the higher plane on which he sometimes used to frisk, he still, also like them, has a grand time of it on the lower one."

At least one modern commentator makes an interesting point, noting that *Topper* was published during a period of prosperity in the United States, whereas *Topper Takes a Trip* appeared at the height of the Depression. And yet the latter contains no reference to the economic climate, despite the title character being a banker, and finds its cast of players frolicking in wealth and luxury on the French Riviera:

"It is as though Topper and his friends exist in a separate world where the stock market never crashed and life continued to roar as it had done in the previous decade. Perhaps that was one reason why Smith chose to set his sequel in France, so that none of the American reality would be forced to intrude itself on his happy company.

"On the other hand, Smith was writing to amuse rather than to depress his readers. People had enough misery in their own lives; they wanted to read about characters who were carefree and unshackled by economic considerations."[42]

For the screen version, producer Hal Roach retained the sympathetic view of France. Mrs. Topper at one point comments, regarding the manners she finds in the country, "Too bad the people in America aren't French." Other than that, the film titled *Topper Takes a Trip* contains no similarity to Thorne Smith's novel. That is perhaps why the story raised only minor objections when submitted for approval by the Production Code Administration. There was, of course, too much drinking and drunkenness, and a scene in which Mrs. Topper's French love interest is buried in the sand minus his bathing trunks caused some concern. Otherwise, Joseph E. Breen at the Production Code Administration was delighted with the film, telegraphing his boss Will H. Hays in New York, "Hal Roach's latest Topper picture is a smash and quite the funniest thing we have seen in many, many months."

Topper was the only one of his novels for which Thorne Smith wrote a sequel. It was also the only one of the screen adaptations to spawn not one but two sequels. As early as the summer of 1937, Hal Roach pointed out that he owned the rights to *Topper Takes a Trip* and that he planned to film it in the near future. Bennett and Norman Z. McLeod were under contract to the studio and available for the sequel, and, as the *Los Angeles Times* (August 25, 1937) pointed out, "Young could probably be had for a price, even if Grant couldn't."

The latter comment proved correct, but no effort was made to replace the actor with another in the same role. Instead, the film began by setting the scene with what had happened in the previous production, with a clip in which Cary Grant appears. The producer noted in the opening titles that "grateful acknowledgement is expressed to Mr. Cary Grant for his consent to the use of scenes from the original *Topper*." Providing Constance Bennett with companionship in lieu of Cary Grant is Skippy, playing Mr. Atlas, the screen equivalent of Oscar, a role initially assigned to Asta, the famous dog from the "Nick and Nora Charles" series. Rounding out the cast, and repeating the substantial role he had in the original film as Wilkins, the butler, is Alan Mowbray.

Shooting took place between August and October 1938. The film was ready for general release in January of the following year. Jack Jevne and Eddie Moran, responsible for the script of *Topper*, returned for the sequel, and they were joined by Corey Ford.

Topper Takes a Trip begins with Topper in the divorce court, where wife Clara accuses him of adultery with the ghost of Marion Kerby. When the case is thrown out of court, Clara is persuaded by her friend Mrs. Parkhurst (played by Verree Teasdale) to sail for France, where a divorce is more likely. Marion Kerby learns of Topper's problems, returns to earth and persuades the banker to head for France in pursuit of his wife.

On the Riviera, Topper and Marion discover that Clara is being pursued by a suave Continental-type in search of money, named Baron de Rossi (and played by Alexander D'Arcy, who had portrayed similar roles in silent films). Thanks to Marion's efforts, Baron de Rossi is routed, at one point (as mentioned above) by the removal of his bathing trunks, and Clara and Cosmo Topper are reconciled. Critics and public alike agreed that the best sequence in the film involved Marion's dancing with Topper and then making herself invisible when Mrs. Topper arrives, leaving

Topper apparently dancing with himself. A series of shots from that sequence was even used to advertise the film.

Topper Takes a Trip received its premiere at Grauman's Chinese Theatre on December 27, 1938. The *Los Angeles Times* the following day complained that the film "does not move quite as easily in certain spots

Former silent leading man Alexander D'Arcy shows off his physique to the delight of Billie Burke and the displeasure of Roland Young in Topper Takes a Trip.

as the original," but noted that Roland Young as Topper "seems due to become a screen institution," and praised Billie Burke, "at her giddy best." The film subsequently opened in March 1939 at Warners Hollywood and Downtown Theatres on a double bill with *Secret Service of the Air*, starring Ronald Reagan.

While not receiving incredibly good reviews, *Topper Takes a Trip* was welcomed by both the trade and general press, as well as by the various women's groups. As with the predecessor, the last were particularly enthusiastic. The California Federation of Business & Professional Women's Clubs described the film as a "Delightful comedy, with adroit photography, excellent acting, expert direction, and clever dialogue." Similarly, the Southern California Council of Federated Church Women hailed

"A lively, highly entertaining and dramatic comedy with a fantastic plot admirably handled, by a popular cast."

The trade paper *The Film Daily* (January 5, 1939) described the film as a "Grand sequel to the first *Topper* comedy with ectoplasm girl bringing delight and laughs." *Variety* (January 4, 1939), having forgotten its negativity towards the first film, was particularly enthusiastic:

"A delightful, very entertaining comedy built around several of the characters who appeared in *Topper*, of which this is a sequel, and so well produced by the Hal Roach plant as to suggest that a cycle based on Topper's experiences should be in order. One a year about Topper and the invisible characters around him, with attendant trick photography and film technique, would no doubt be welcomed by the exhibitors...

"The picture will do equally well in the small towns as in the big, and is a natural for world consumption. Foreign territories will go for it as quickly as the domestic field in view of its universal appeal and the simple but high[ly] effective story."

In *The New Yorker* (January 7, 1939), John Mosher echoed *Variety's* comments: "I myself could easily stand a *Topper* a year, and I might easily be persuaded to go to a revival of *The Invisible Man* as well." Some of the critics complained of the absence of Cary Grant, while others felt that there was a limit to the uses to which the special effects might be put. Howard Barnes, writing in the *New York Herald Tribune* (December 30, 1938) thought the film only "a moderately beguiling comic fantasy." In the *New York Times* (December 30, 1938), Frank S. Hugent saw "a case where the spirits are willing but the freshness is weak. Mr. Smith's lively spooks can defy some natural laws by remaining on earth in a state of transient translucence, but the law of diminishing returns is one not even a dematerialized terrier can romp through." *Photoplay* (March 1939) unfairly accused the Production Code Administration of having removed the spice from the program, with "only whimsy left." *Time* (January 9, 1939) devoted considerable space to an analysis of the film, concluding,

"Admirers of the late Thorne Smith...will doubtless be enchanted by the gaiety and humor of these proceedings. Less prejudiced cinemaddicts may feel that the comic possibilities of its trick photography are less inexhaustible than its producers supposed. Once the side-splitting spectacle of doors opening without apparent human aid has lost its novelty, the picture's only surprises are occasional droll antics by Actors Young and Burke, and a few scraps of bright dialogue."

TOPPER RETURNS

Hal Roach returned to Topper for one last outing with the appositely named *Topper Returns*, shot late in 1940 and released in March 1941. While both Roland Young and Billie Burke return to reprise their original

Joan Blondell, Roland Young and Carole Landis in Topper Returns.

roles, the film is not based on anything by Thorne Smith, but is strictly a comedy-mystery by screenwriters Jonathan Latimer and Gordon Douglas. The former was the author of a number of mystery novels, while Douglas was primarily a director, long associated with Hal Roach and responsible for some of the "Our Gang" comedies. The emphasis is on mystery in the style of the "old dark house" films, such as the 1932 James Whale production of the same title and the silent 1927 feature, *The Cat and the Canary*. Unfortunately, the mystery is rather stereotyped and the comedy sluggish. The film is a hybrid. After some consideration, the trade paper *Motion Picture Daily* (March 12, 1941) opined, "Best sold as a comedy." There are many who would disagree with this opinion.

The storyline concerns the return from China of two young ladies, Gail Richards and Ann Carrington, played respectively by Joan Blondell and Carole Landis. Carrington is about to claim her inheritance at the spooky Carrington residence. Her friend is mistaken for her and murdered, and the villain eventually identified as the man claiming to be Ann Carrington's father but in reality his business partner. Topper first meets the ladies when their car crashes and he gives them a ride, with

Topper Returns: *Eddie "Rochester" Anderson, as Eddie the chauffeur, displays the appropriate regard for Mr. and Mrs. Topper.*

Gail Richard's perched on his lap. "Danger ahead — two of 'em," warns his chauffeur. It is the ghostly Gail who forces Topper to investigate her murder and uncover the villain.

There is a nice touch in having the villain attempt to escape by car and crashing at the same spot where the Kerbys were killed. He even sits on the same log from the original production, along with Gail and the Topper chauffeur. Earlier, Topper had made reference to the Kerbys when telling the ghostly Gail that "I've had enough trouble with your kind of people."

Eddie "Rochester" Anderson is cast as the chauffeur, which, of course, allows for appropriate, period racist humor. Anderson is best remembered as Jack Benny's manservant, and at one point in the film he threatens Mrs.

Topper, "I'm going back to Mr. Benny." As the villain, H.B. Warner gives a good performance, as do the two leading ladies, with Joan Blondell obviously getting the best scenes and attention. Blondell has been a fixture at Warner Bros. in the 1930s, and joining her as director is another Warner Bros. regular, Roy Del Ruth, who, based on previous efforts, presumably brings more drama and less comedy to the production.

Aside from a chauffeur, the Toppers also acquire a maid for Mrs. Topper, played by Patsy Kelly. Supporting villainous roles are handled by Trevor Bardette as Rama, the Carrington's butler, Rafaela Ottiano as the Carrington housekeeper and George Zucco as Dr. Jeris. Dennis O'Keefe, as the cab driver bringing the two women to the Carrington home, provides adequate romantic interest for Carole Landis.

The script presented no problems for the Production Code Administration, with only minor changes required, involving Eddie "Rochester" Anderson's diving under a bed and apparently bumping into a chamber pot, and facetious references to presidential hopeful Wendell Wilkie. The film was not well received on the East Coast. In *The New Yorker* (March 29, 1941), John Mosher wrote that it "strives less for laughs than it does for the mystery killings, sliding panels, hands in the dark, trapdoors, and so on of the orthodox thriller." When *Topper Returns* opened at the Capitol Theatre in New York, Theodore Strauss in the *New York Times* (March 28, 1941) described it as "a rather sluggish ghost-hunt," adding, "even a ghost may become a common bore if it stays around too long…one may raise a ghost, but hardly the ghost of a ghost."

Even the trade papers were unenthused. *Variety* (March 12, 1941) described *Topper Returns* as "far short of its predecessors in ingenuity and that reasonable plausibility which is necessary to get over the fantastic idea that the spirit of the dead enjoy the discomfiture of the living."

The only positive review came from Edwin Schallert in the *Los Angeles Times* (March 12, 1941). His opinion was that, "*Topper Returns* is high-power fun for the devotees of mystery melodramas. It is better in this respect than either of its predecessors, despite the fact that it gets farther away from the Thorne Smith original." The only problem with Schallert's comment is that, of course, the Thorne Smith original was not a mystery melodrama, and thus a sequel in this genre will of necessity be better than its predecessors in another.

At least one modern commentator has described *Topper Returns* as the character's "best cinematic outing."[43] He is, however, probably in the minority in that it is difficult to find anything of Thorne Smith here and little that constitutes a good comedy or a good mystery. It is too derivative of other films and at times too convoluted for its own good. Even Roland Young seems out-of-place, although Billie Burke more than excels as his much maligned wife who has no problem in taking care of herself, harshly describing her husband as "a paunchy, middle-aged man." That same paunch is also referenced by George Kerby in *Topper Takes a Trip.*

Unlike his ghosts, Topper did not die with *Topper Returns,* but continued on, first with a radio series in 1945, and then with a television series on CBS from October 1953 through September 1955. Topper was played in the television series by Leo G. Carroll with the husband-and-wife team of Anne Jeffreys and Robert Sterling playing Marion and George Kerby. Mrs. Topper, renamed Henrietta, was played by Lee Patrick. Thorne Smith would have been delighted with the addition of a ghostly St. Bernard who enjoys getting drunk on his own "Good Samaritan" brandy. Smith's storyline was changed in that the Kerbys had been killed by an avalanche while on a skiing trip to Europe. Also killed was their would-be rescuer, Neil, the St. Bernard. The three return to the United States to discover that the Kerby home is now owned by the Toppers. A regular writer on the series was Stephen Sondheim, prior to his success as a lyricist and composer of legendary proportion.

The primary writer on the *Topper* series, who also served as story editor and occasional director, was Philip Rapp (1907-1966). It was Rapp who was responsible for Neil, the St. Bernard, and who also brought in George Oppenheimer as a regular writer on the show, which was sponsored by R. J. Reynolds. Interestingly, Rapp also worked at some point post-1962 on a television version of *The Stray Lamb,* but nothing came of the project.

Topper was greeted with a rave review in *Variety* (October 14, 1953), which commented that Carroll was "the most logical successor to the late Roland Young," and praised "a slick cast paced into an ectoplastic winner." The first episode featured veteran actor Lyle Talbott as a real estate agent selling the Kerby home, and the series also began with a couple of other great character actors in supporting roles, Kathleen Freeman as Katie the maid and Thurston Hall as Mr. Schuyler.

Anne Jeffreys has vivid memories of the television series. "As a little girl, I had seen the movies, and who could not love them," she recalled.[44] She and Robert Sterling had been on a nightclub tour and were playing at the Sands Hotel in Las Vegas when their agent telephoned. He asked if the couple was interested in a television version of *Topper*, they responded, "absolutely," and after arrival in Los Angeles for a nighttime personal appearance at the Coconut Grove, Jeffreys and Sterling filmed the pilot during the day. From Los Angeles, the couple moved on to the Fairmont Hotel in San Francisco, and there they received another telephone call from their agent telling them to cancel the remainder of the tour. The pilot had taken only two weeks to be sold.

Filming *Topper* was "a wonderful time in our lives," remembers Jeffreys. Of Leo G. Carroll, she says, "We loved him. There was such rapport... We did own a piece of them," she notes in reference to the rights to the series, but eventually after ten years of litigation the couple finished up with nothing. The series has long disappeared from television.

Less successful than the series was a television movie, *Topper*, which first aired on ABC on November 9, 1979. The two-hour show featured Jack Warden as Topper, Rue McClanahan as Clara Topper, with then husband-and-wife team Kate Jackson and Andrew Stevens not only as the Kerbys but also serving as executive producers. Charles S. Dubin directed. Since the television movie, there have been rumors of a feature film with Tom Cruise and Julia Roberts, and also a stage play, but nothing has transpired.

It would be remiss not to note that Topper lived on not as a banker, not even as a dog, but as a horse. In sixty-six feature films and fifty-two television shows, Hopalong Cassidy's horse was named Topper. He was given the name in 1937 by Grace Bradley, whose husband William Boyd played Hopalong Cassidy, because the lady had a fondness for Cosmo Topper. Topper, the horse, not the banker who will never leave us, died in 1961 at the age of twenty-six.[45]

1. Joseph Leo Blotner, Thorne Smith: A Study in Popular Fiction, pp. 66-67.

2. Did She Fall?, p. 7.

3. Ibid, p. 1.

4. Gary Hoppenstand, "Murder and Other Acts of High Society," p. 63.

5. Roland Young and Thorne Smith among Others, Thorne Smith: His Life and Times, p. 27.

6. Topper, p. 8.

7. Ibid, p. 3.

8. Ibid, p. 8.

9. Ibid, p. 12.

10. Ibid, p. 53.

11. Ibid, p. 17.

12. Ibid, p. 23.

13. Ibid, p. 47.

14. Ibid, p. 215.

15. Ibid, p. 209.

16. Quoted in the biographical note to the Modern Library edition of Topper, p. vi.

17. Grace Kingsley, "Hobnobbing in Hollywood," Los Angeles Times, February 27, 1933, p. A9.

18. Elizabeth Ward interview, Topper program note, Los Angeles County Museum of Art screening, 1976.

19. Information is taken from the Hal Roach Collection, Cinema Library, University of Southern California.

20. Carolyn See, Introduction to Topper, p. ix.

21. That copy of Topper is for sale, as I write, from Royal Books of Baltimore, Maryland; the price is $15,000.00.

22. Joseph Blotner to Anthony Slide, September 1, 2009.

23. Roland Young is also the author of two other published volumes: a collection of caricatures titled Actors and Others (Pascal Covici, 1925) and an anthology of poetry titled Not for Children (Doubleday, Doran, 1930, reprinted 1945).

24. Roland Young's unpublished, untitled and unpaged autobiography.

25. Ibid.

26. John Scott, "Amazing New Camera Tricks Developed by Screen Magicians," Los Angeles Times, April 25, 1937, p. C1.

27. This and other correspondence taken from the Production Code Administration file on Topper, Margaret Herrick Library, Academy of Motion Picture Arts and Sciences.

28. In the novel, Topper is described as "Nearly forty and acquiring flesh," p. 40, which Young is not.

29. Apparently, the exterior entrance of the Bullocks Wilshire Department Store on Wilshire Boulevard, near downtown Los Angeles, stood in for the entrance to the Seabreeze Hotel.

30. Some of Marvin Hatley's music cues in Topper are also to be heard in another Hal Roach production of the same year, Way out West, starring Laurel and Hardy.

31. Joseph Leo Blotner, Thorne Smith: A Study in Popular Fiction, p. 34.

32. Quoted in Joseph Leo Blotner, Thorne Smith: A Study in Popular Fiction, p. 102.

33. Quoted in Joseph Leo Blotner, Thorne Smith: A Study in Popular Fiction, p. 33.

34. Topper Takes a Trip, p.1.

35. In the original manuscript, Thorne Smith has Oscar lifting his leg at each tree in the principality. When Colonel Scott comments, "he's merely expressing his opinion of Monaco," Topper responds, "Far more precisely that we have been able to do." Joseph Lee Blotner, Thorne Smith: A Study in Popular Fiction, p. 112.

36. Topper Takes a Trip, p. 159.

37. Ibid, p. 265.

38. Ibid, p. 307.

39. Ibid, pp. 310-311.

40. Ibid, p. 309.

41. Ibid, p. 312.

42. Stephen Goldin, "Topper and Topper Takes a Trip," p. 1961.

43. Ken Hanke, 'Topper Returns," p. 54.

44. This and other quotes from a January 26, 2010 telephone conversation with Anthony Slide.

45. As documented in Petrine Day Mitchum with Audrey Pavia, Hollywood Hoofbeats: Trails Blazed across the Silver Screen, Irvine, Ca.: Bowtie Press, 2005, p. 99.

CHAPTER THREE

THE NIGHT LIFE
OF THE GODS

Topper was not the first of Thorne Smith's novels to be filmed. That honor goes to *The Night Life of the Gods*, published by Doubleday, Doran in 1931, immediately after *Did She Fall?* It was another major American humorist, Ogden Nash, who had been responsible for Smith's coming to what was to be his publisher for the remainder of Smith's career. As a young editor with Doubleday, Doran, Nash visited Smith at Free Acres and persuaded him to sign a contract. As Nash recalled for Joseph Blotner, "I had been an ardent admirer of his since reading *Topper*. I heard rumors that he was not happy with his current publishers...I got hold of Thorne, we saw eye to eye about many things, and it didn't take too much persuasion to add him to the Doubleday list...He was very quiet, almost neurotically shy. A little faded wisp of a man with pale golden hair, usually dressed in brown, who reminded me of an Autumn; always carried a stout cane as if to avoid being blown away. Sweet, but you felt an other-world, changeling quality."[1]

Ogden Nash left Doubleday, Doran shortly thereafter to join the staff of *The New Yorker*. Smith's new editor was Malcolm Johnson, who writes fondly, perceptively and semi-anonymously of the novelist in the thirty-two page monograph *Thorne Smith: His Life and Times*, published as a promotional tool by Doubleday, Doran. Johnson had previously been responsible for the "Crime Club," one of fifteen book clubs owned by Doubleday, Doran. He was to become executive vice president of the company before his early death, at the age of fifty-five, in February 1958.

Thorne Smith was not the only comic writer of his generation to be published by Doubleday, Doran. In 1924, prior to the merger of the two companies, Doran published P.G. Wodehouse's seminal work, and the source for so many sequel volumes, *Jeeves*. As one reviewer, Harry

Emerson Wildes, wrote in the *Philadelphia Public-Ledger*, "When I come to be dictator I'm going to have all books burned but Thorne Smith's and Wodehouse's. Then we'll rebuild civilization anew with them as a basis and we'll have Utopia."[2] It would have been a Utopia that would have made Doubleday, Doran wealthy.

It might be argued that the two Topper books are concerned with living beyond one's time in that the ghosts are permitted to continue existence on earth albethey dead. In *The Night Life of the Gods*, Thorne Smith deals more directly with the same issue, although, as might be expected, the approach is far from ponderous. *The Night Life of the Gods* begins with the dedication, "To borrow from Mr. J.B. Priestley this book is in gratitude offered to a couple of good companions Neal and Dorothy Andrews." The reference to the British writer, whose novel, *The Good Companions*, became both a play and a film is the first of two literary allusions in the book. A few pages later, Smith makes reference to his hero's laboratory, "filled with more than enough instruments and paraphernalia to satiate the lust for descriptive detail of an avalanche of Sinclair Lewises."[3]

This was not the first time that Smith had experimented with literary references. In a paragraph, subsequently deleted from *Topper Takes a Trip*, he had a character comment, "Wish to God Michael Arlen or Scott Fitzgerald would put words in your various mouths…I don't know why I listen but I do. This doesn't sound like the smart sophisticated Riviera one reads so much about."[4]

The central character in *The Night Life of the Gods* is a thirty-seven-year-old bachelor with black hair and lean, angular features named Hunter Hawk, a wealthy, amateur scientist, whose home has been taken over by his sister, Alice Lambert's family, consisting of husband, son and daughter, and grandpa. Aside from daughter Daphne, known as Daffy, they are an obnoxious group, interested only in inheriting Hawk's wealth. Their plans are thwarted when Hawk discovers how to turn a human body to stone and back again, using two rings, one emitting a white ray turning flesh to stone and the other reversing the process with a green ray. The first recipient of his invention is the tail of his dog Blotto, which is quickly returned to normal. Less fortunate are the Lamberts who are transformed to stone by a vengeful Hawk, who is delighted when Blotto raises his leg against the feet and legs of the statue-like nephew.

That evening, Hawk goes out for a walk and meets a "little tattered man," who is bereft at the sight of a scarecrow wearing clothes better than his, and who reveals himself as one of the last leprechauns. As the man explains, "We emigrated from Ireland long before the great-great-grandfather of Christopher Columbus ever climbed through a bedroom window...

"The country virtually belonged to us then. We didn't have to listen to 'Mother Machree' or 'Come Back to Erin' or 'The rose of Sharon,' or to any bum jokes about It Seems There Were Two Irishmen, Pat and Mike. Taking the good with the bad, we were quite happy and contented. In later years the uninterrupted wailing of those songs over on the other side was one of the reasons for our migration...Everything went along well until the police force came over from Ireland...Our magic gradually weakened...Most of our people have moved away to China or to South America for the revolutions. Many of them just crawled into caves and crevasses in rocks and went to sleep forever."[5]

Just as Irish cops are the bane of the little man's existence, so often do they appear to play a comic-villainous part in many of Smith's works.

The little man, who since the war has called himself Ludwig Turner, takes Hawk to meet his daughter Megaera or Meg, who is a direct descendent of one of the Three Furies and who also has the magic to turn statues into real people and back again. Meg places her seal on Hawk and accompanies him to his home and to his bed. Blotto's snores are a problem, but then as Smith notes, "Between Blotto and his uninvited bedfellow there was scarcely any sleep at all for Hunter Hawk that night."[6]

The following day, the entire family, restored to human form, along with Meg, attends church, and the visit concludes with the vicar's buttocks turned to stone. Somehow the reader immediately knows that a visit to church by Thorne Smith characters will not end happily. Next, Hawk, Meg, Daffy, and her boyfriend, Cyril Sparks, a dull fellow but fond of his liquor and therefore acceptable to Hawk, are invited by an amorous neighbor to a party, where Hawk spends time semi-nude, wearing only a towel, and also turns himself into a statue to avoid having to explain to the neighbor's husband why he is in her bedroom.

Hawk suggests that Meg, Daffy and Cyril set out in his roadster to seek adventure, which involves a visit to a nightspot and an obligatory encounter with the police. Three nights follow in hiding with Meg's father. Daffy and Cyril return to their respective homes, Hawk acquires a long, false beard, and he and Meg set out for New York, along with Betts, the manservant. It is exactly half-way through the novel that Hawk and Meg visit the Metropolitan Museum of Art, with the former using his position and wealth to allow his remaining there after it has closed. Meg is not a great admirer of the classical sculptures; as she tells Hawk, she has a liking for an old boy named Rodin:

"A clever devil, He never bores me. Why? Because he didn't give everything. Always held a little back — suggested something beyond the mere medium in which he worked. He leads us along and points out the rest of the way, but he doesn't take us there and plop us down as if to say, 'Here you are, damn you. This is good. Like it or be forever lost.' No, Rodin holds out and gives our brains a chance to shift gears for themselves."[7]

For Meg suddenly to become an art critic is odd, as odd, in fact, as Thorne Smith's suddenly getting serious and discussing the world of modern sculpture in such a tone.

The sculptures that come to life in *The Night Life of the Gods* are introduced in chapter eight, "The Gods Step Down," and they are motley crew selected by Hawk for transfiguration. Mercury is first. Next, Hawk has in mind Jupiter, but Mercury dissuades him, noting that he is "Too stuffy."[8] The final choices are Bacchus, Neptune, Apollo, Hebe, Perseus (the snakes writhing on the head of Medusa that he is holding cause some trouble), Diana, and Venus. The last is fitted with arms made from putty or plaster-of-paris by Meg. Hawk takes his motley band of naked and semi-naked ex-statues to a department store he knows, where they are suitably clothed. Next, the group is installed at a hotel, where again Hawk and his money are well known and welcome. In her bedroom, Hebe discovers a large "cup" in a cupboard next to the bed, allowing for some chamber pot humor. A fish restaurant is the next stop, with Neptune's attempting to eat live, uncooked lobsters, and where a major fight erupts with fish as the weapons of choice. It becomes a Mack Sennett comedy set in the Fulton Fish Market. Mercury finds a cow and adds it to the group, who return to the hotel for more alcohol, a little sleep, and a disastrous visit to the basement swimming pool and Turkish baths.

The gods indulge in most un-godlike behavior at the Hawk mansion, again, as in previous episodes, reverting to type. A private investigator, hired by Hawk's relatives arrives, along with state troopers, and the gods are carted off to jail. In court, Neptune is mistaken for Hawk. The head of Medusa, complete with snakes, helps clear the building, leaving only the Olympians, Hawk, Meg and Betts. One by one, the gods admit they are tired of the modern world and would prefer to return, as statues, to their plinths. "The world was too much with them, or after them."[9] Or as Meg puts it, "In a world that has forgotten how to play there was no room for the Olympians."[10] After returning the gods to stone, Hawk takes Meg in his arms, kisses her and transforms them both to stone. "Your lips on mine...Always,"[11] she says.

The Night Life of the Gods contains one political comment. When Alice Lambert's husband, Alfred, suggests selling Hawk's invention to the U.S. government as a war weapon, his brother-in-law responds, "But why don't you try to sell it to Mussolini first? He'd put his country in hock to see himself as a statue and to experience while still alive something approaching the adulation of posterity."[12] The novel treats religion with ridicule. Daffy welcomes the opportunity to attend church in that it presents the excuse to "Snaffle down some food and try a glass of wine."[13] Meg is delighted with the opportunity that it provides to steal from the collection plate. The church is described by Thorne Smith as

"one of those fashionable churches one occasionally finds in a semi-suburban community largely inhabited by snobs. It was smart to be seen there occasionally. Members were forever returning to it from Palm Beach, Deauville, St. Moritz, or Park Avenue. It was their way of officially registering the fact that after having spent oodles of money in fashionable travel they were once more honoring the neighborhood with their presence from the upholstered seclusion of their country estates."[14]

Shortly before Hawk takes pity on the vicar and restores his backside to normal, the man announces that he now feels closer to God and that the latter seems much more human. "Previously I believed that the majority of the members of my congregation...did not need saving. Now I feel that they are not worth saving."[15]

Perhaps the most curious aspect of *The Night Life of the Gods* is how entertaining the first half is, and how tedious it becomes once the gods are made human. There is not much originality in their approach to modern society. All they do, basically, is drink and perform the sort of stunts one might expect from drunkards. *The Night Life of the Gods* is one of Thorne Smith's better books because of the early situations and characterizations, but relatively poor in the ultimate premise to which it builds. Scott Veale has commented that "The joke is that the gods are really overgrown children: guileless, bickering and relentless in pursuit of their appetites."[16] The problem is that just as the gods are like children, so are the gags and comic situations equally juvenile.

Contemporary reviews were mixed. The critic in *The Bookman* (May 1931) wrote, "Part farce, part comedy, part satire, reminiscent of *The Wizard of Oz* as well as of more mature humor, the book becomes wearisome before it is finished…some of it is very funny." In the *New York Herald Tribune Books* (March 29, 1931), F.H. Britten commented, "Where *Topper* and *Stray Lamb* were full of sage and varied reports of the ways of man in these times, *The Night Life of the Gods* is more meager by far; it is almost completely committed to irresponsible nonsense — a nonsense which, delectable though it is, grows monotonous for want of the occasional infusion of a bit of matter-of-fact sense." More positive was the *New York Times* (March 29, 1931), whose reviewer wrote, "This hilarious interlude of the gods is not without salt. Wit tumbles merrily and the ways of both man and god receive salutary criticisms."

At least one modern critic has described *The Night Life of the Gods* as being "particularly wild and shambolic in its comedy."[17] Whether the novel is more over the top than its predecessors or those that followed is open to question. Certainly, everyone in the story is irresponsible on a level scarcely to be comprehensible to the average reader.

The Night Life of the Gods had a surprising admirer in composer George Gershwin. On June 12, 1931, he wrote to the author,

"I am reading with great pleasure your book, *Night Life of the Gods* and find that it has qualities which appeal to me very much.

"It seems to me that anyone who can write such a fanciful tale, with such witty dialogue, might be able to write a very interesting libretto for a play with music, along the same lines.

"If you will be good enough to call me…I would like to make an appointment with you to talk over the possibilities of such an idea."[18]

The record is silent as to whether the two men ever met and, if so, what transpired. Interestingly, the 1943 Kurt Weill musical, *One Touch of Venus*, with lyrics by Ogden Nash, takes as its theme the transformation to human life of a statue of Venus, the Goddess of Love. The source for the musical, however, is not Thorne Smith, but rather F. Anstey and his 1885 novel, *Tinted Venus: A Farcical Romance*.

Screen rights to *The Night Life of the Gods* were acquired for $3,500.00 in March 1934 by Universal Pictures Corp., which dropped the definite article from its release title. Realizing the name recognition of the author, Universal ultimately billed the film on its main title as "Thorne Smith's *Night Life of the Gods*." It is a nice touch that the title also flashes on and off rather in the fashion of a neon sign. None of the players is listed on the main title card, with the "mortals" noted in order of importance on one card and the gods and goddesses on another. The studio hired a group of sculptors to work on the statues — five according to *Daily Variety* (August 8, 1934) and eleven according to the *Los Angeles Times* (August 26, 1934). "All the nudes will have to wear something," reported the latter.

To adapt the Thorne Smith novel, Universal assigned Barry Trivers, who was under contract to the studio at that time but who had worked on only three earlier feature-length screenplays. Trivers (1907-1981) was to be a prolific screenwriter, moving from Universal to M-G-M, and embarking on a lengthy television career from the early 1950s through into the mid 1970s. Prior to his screen career, Trivers had been an actor on Broadway and written songs and sketches for the 1931 edition of the *Ziegfeld Follies*. He wrote the 1947 musical comedy *Heaven on Earth*, authored a novel, and wrote a number of songs, including "Do the New York." Playing the leading character of Meg in the film is Trivers' wife, Florine McKinney.

Barry Trivers was quite obviously a sophisticate and someone who would have felt comfortable with the Thorne Smith assignment. It might even be argued that it was his most prominent screen work in that his obituaries all identified him as having been responsible for "adapting Thorne Smith's book."

As might be expected, the initial script raised immediate concern from the Production Code Administration. James Wingate wrote to Harry Zehner at Universal on July 2, 1934, noting that he had read the script,

"and take this opportunity of expressing to you our deep concern over a good deal of the material treated in the story While we wish to compliment you on the manner in which the book from which this script is adapted has been treated and modified from our point of view, we feel that this version of the story still suggests material objection from the point of view of nudity and suggestiveness."

Five pages of deletions and modifications were included in the letter.

Various conferences with director Lowell Sherman took place between July and September 1934, and the Production Code Administration staff viewed a "rough print." The final version of the film was viewed on November 13, 1934, and some dialogue cuts were required as well as the deletion of the gods "using the bed pot." A beer stein was substituted — not presumably for the same use. The film was finally approved for release on December 5, 1934, when Certification No. 470 was issued. However, the Production Code Administration staff was still nervous about the film and reviewed it yet again on December 28, 1934.

The production was budgeted at $350,000.00. Filming had taken place between August 13 and November 15, 1934. Director Lowell Sherman (1885-1934) had made his screen debut as a splendidly wicked villain in D.W. Griffith's *Way Down East* (1920) before turning to directing in 1930. He was very much a sophisticate with a healthy appetite for sex; in fact, he was with Roscoe "Fatty" Arbuckle in 1921 at the San Francisco hotel where Virginia Rappe died, leading to the comedian's manslaughter charge. Claiming that the sets were too hot, apparently, Sherman liked to direct in his underwear, something of which I am sure Thorne Smith would have approved. *Night Life of the Gods* was to be Lowell Sherman's last film; he died shortly after begining production on his next, the first full-color Technicolor feature, *Becky Sharp*.

A contemporary report in the *New York Times* provides a good portrait of Sherman's directorial methods on *Night Life of the Gods*:

"The Thorne Smith story has, of course, been purified with great liberality, but out of it, indications are, has come a rollicking comedy.

"Mr. Sherman works with astounding ease in directing his picture. He seems to pay no attention to anything. To quote him, his instructions to his players are, 'Enter here. Exit there. Camera!' He says that he is too old to teach youngsters how to act and too young to presume to tell troupers what to do. He rarely photographs a scene more than twice, generally but once. He spends most of his time off stage chatting with friends while the camera and electrical crews arrange the settings. Then, at the sound of his assistant's whistle, he enters the scene, orders the cameras to roll, decides instantly whether the 'take' is successful, and with happy nonchalance resumes his conversation."[19]

Alan Mowbray, later to be associated with the "Topper" films, plays Hunter Hawk, and looks perhaps somewhat older than the reader might take the hero to be. Supporting Mowbray are relatively little known players, including the aforementioned Florine McKinney as Meg, Ferdinand Gottschalk as her father, and Peggy Shannon as Daphne Lambert. From the silent era, when he had been a child actor playing opposite Mary Pickford, is Wesley Barry as Daphne's disagreeable brother. There are a couple of familiar names among the gods and goddeses, but they also are portrayed by little known performers: Raymond Benard as Apollo, George

Hassell as Bacchus, Irene Ware as Diana, Geneva Mitchell as Hebe, Paul Kaye as Mercury, Robert Warwick as Neptune, Pat De Cicco as Perseus, and Marda Deering as Venus. At least Universal did not attempt to cut costs by reducing the number of Olympians. According to publicity, Lowell Sherman selected the actors and actresses on the basis of their similarity in appearance to the gods and goddesses. How he knew what they looked like is not recorded. Pat De Cicco was actually a Hollywood agent. Raymond Benard was a physical education instructor who changed his name to Ray "Crash" Corrigan and starred in a number of serials and "B" Westerns.

Just as the main title acknowledged the author of the original novel, so did the foreword to the film pay tribute to its source:

"Once upon a time, a famous author named Thorne Smith wrote a book, conceived in a moment of delicious delirium, and written in a cuckoo clock. The first chapters convinced us *he* was crazy. The ensuing left doubt that possibly *we* were. So we leave you to enjoy this new and completely mad type of whimsical humor on the screen. Stop rattling cellophane! Take Sonny's shoes off! Park your gum under the seat where it belongs, and let's all go crazy together."

The foreword is an effort to match Thorne Smith whimsy for whimsy. Unfortunately, it does not really succeed. But that is not because it fails to try. The film is, almost surprisingly, good, retaining much of Thorne Smith's dialogue and humor and at times besting the novel.

Night Life of the Gods follows the book fairly closely. It begins with the explosions from Hunter Hawk's experiments, the relatives believing he is dead, discussing what they might do with his estate and Hawk's appearance very much alive. The inventor is, in fact, up in the rafters, where he has been blown by the explosion. With the help of niece Daphne he descends without the aid of a ladder in what is presented as a circus act, with appropriate musical accompaniment. (Praise must go to composer Arthur Morton for a delightful theme tune played throughout the film and which remains with the viewer long after the final scene.) Both Hawk and Daphne are knocked unconscious and found by Meg, here the daughter of the gardener. A simplistic special effects trick involving circling lights indicates to the sophisticated viewer at least that everything that follows is a dream — in other words, the storyline of the novel.

Hawk demonstrates his ability to turn individuals to stone, first the tail of Blotto the dog, then himself and finally the family. The Production

Code Administration would not permit Blotto's lifting of his leg but he does sniff around the nephew's stone foot. After the meeting with Meg and her father, Hawk and she do spend the night together, but, following the Production Code Administration requirement, sleeping fully clothed in separate chairs rather than beds. A sequence in a night-

Hunter Hawk demonstrates his ability to turn himself into stone in front of his relatives played by, from left to right, Theresa Maxwell Conover, Peggy Shannon, Richard Carle, Phillips Smalley, and Wesley Barry.

club is one of the funniest and most enjoyable in the film as Florine McKinney and Alan Mowbray dance together, with the latter adopting the most extraordinary of facial expressions. Hawk and company move to New York and he and Meg visit the Museum. Hawk muses on what the gods might do "If they were alive today," and the transformations take place. Hawk considers "humanizing" the Three Graces, but when he discovers that they become a trio singing popular songs, he reverses the process.

Of the gods, it is Bacchus who is the most entertaining and given the best lines. The others are all really very much supporting players, although Hebe's desperate search for cups to hold is somewhat entertaining. Diana is seen in human form only from the neck up until Meg drapes her upper body using the long flowing robe that the goddess is wearing.

There are scenes taken from the novel in the department store, in the hotel and its swimming pool and at the fish market. At the hotel, two matrons coming out of the elevator look with distaste at the gods and

Florine McKinney as Meg helps actress Marda Deering as Diana appear both armless and respectably clothed.

remark, "Motion picture people." The slapstick sequence with fish replacing pies actually works better on screen than in the novel.

Once the gods have been transformed back into statues and Hawk has turned himself, alongside Meg, into a statue, the same special effects (if such they can be called) that began the dream sequence end it. Hawk is in an ambulance in the company of Meg and Betts the butler. "I've had a horrible dream," he tells them. Audience might well disagree — the dream has been far from horrible and the film far from disappointing.

Did the story need to be told as a dream? In one major respect it did, for Hawk makes over-judicious use of the ring, and there are too many individuals turned, it would appear, permanently to stone. For example, the relatives are not turned back as they are in the novel. Only one detective, Mulligan, played by William (Stage) Boyd, becomes human again, with the explanation that he suffers from gallstones.

Presumably, the Production Code Administration again stepped in at the conclusion of the dream, and while Hawk and Meg are transformed

George Hassell as an ebullient Bacchus with Florine McKinney as Meg.

to stone, they are simply sitting next to each other, seated on a plinth. There is no kiss for eternity.

In that trade reviewers, aside from *Variety*'s critic, comment that the film ends with the couple turned to stone, it is possible that Universal added the ending in the ambulance. But, if this is true, it would mean that a scene earlier in the film would have to have been reshot, and the footage showing Meg's father as nothing more than a gardener was superfluous. It is obvious that more scenes were shot than those to be found in the film, but, happily, the studio had the good sense to keep the running time to seventy-three entertaining minutes.

Reviewers were quick to point out the limitations of the screen adaptation. Recognizing that it was not easy to film the Thorne Smith novel, *Variety* (February 27, 1935) acknowledged that "Universal has made an acceptable version…Not an easy matter but it has managed to keep in the fun and restrain it from getting too rough." Another trade paper, *Motion Picture Daily* (December 8, 1934) described the film as "completely but pleasantly goofy." The day after the film's New York opening at the Roxy, Andre Sennwald in the *New York Times* (February 23, 1935) wrote that

Geneva Mitchell as Hebe is caught trying to steal cups from the restaurant.

if it "lacks much of the heady merriment which distinguished the original…it is probably because the eye is a more prosaic instrument than the unfettered imagination.

"Somehow the petrified humans and the revivified gods and goddesses are not as devastatingly mirthful as they seemed under the hypnosis of Mr. Smith's antic prose.

"Once you accept that natural limitation, you are likely to find that the late Lowell Sherman has performed an amusing and occasionally hilarious screen transformation of the novel…only moderately entertaining. One of the disadvantages is that the current cinema morality has forced Mr. Sherman to abandon most of the ribald humor of the original."

The other New York critics were equally restrained in their commentary. The *Journal* described the film as "conventional boisterous slapstick." The *Sun* thought it, "Not as funny as it should be." The *World-Telegram* dismissed the film as "muddled and sluggish," while the *Herald-Tribune* found it "chiefly results in futility."

A scene familiar to readers of the novel but not to be found in the release version of Night Life of the Gods: *left to right, Gilbert Emery as Betts, Alan Mowbray as Hunter Hawk, Florine McKinney as Meg, and Irene Ware as Diana.*

After the February 26, 1935 Los Angeles opening at the Pantages Theatre in Hollywood, Philip K. Scheuer in the *Los Angeles Times* (February 28, 1935) acknowledged that Universal had "done what it could" in transferring the novel to the screen. "At certain moments, Thorne Smith's fun comes through. These are moments when, by a happy coincidence, acting, direction, movement and dialogue achieve a spontaneous homogeneity — click! click! click! like that. When this happens, we chuckle. For the rest, the laughs are so scattered that you will seldom hear two persons responding at the same instant"

Universal's screen rights to the novel were limited to a number of years, which perhaps explains the low price paid up-front. Because the studio no longer has ownership of the underlying story, *Night Life of the Gods* has not been seen publicly for many years, and is considered almost a "lost" film, although a fine grain master is held by the UCLA Film and Television Archive. In the 1970s, the motion picture rights to the novel were acquired from the Thorne Smith estate by Tim McHugh. McHugh is ideally suited to produce a new version in that his background is in visual effects, and very obviously new technologies will be of inestimable value in bringing the gods back to life and dealing with the problem of Venus de Milo's lack of arms. Unfortunately, to date, the Hollywood studios have displayed no interest in the remake and it remains as much a dream as the story in the Universal adaptation proved to be.

1. Joseph Leo Blotner, Thorne Smith: A Study in Popular Fiction, p. 30.

2. Quoted in Roland Young and Thorne Smith among Others, Thorne Smith: His Life and Times, p. 10.

3. The Night Life of the Gods, p. 10.

4. Joseph Leo Blotner, Thorne Smith: A Study in Popular Fiction, p. 122.

5. The Night Life of the Gods, pp. 44-45.

6. Ibid, p. 73.

7. Ibid, p. 154.

8. Ibid, p. 164.

9. Ibid, p. 306.

10. Ibid, p. 310.

11. Ibid, p. 310.

12. Ibid, p. 35.

13. Ibid, p. 81.

14. Ibid, p. 82-83.

15. Ibid, p. 277.

16. Scott Veale, "Drinking Gin with the Dead," p. 47.

17. David Langford, "Smith, (James) Thorne (Jr.)," p. 881.

18. Joseph Leo Blotner, Thorne Smith: A Study in Popular Fiction, p. 60; the original letter had survived in the papers owned by Thorne Smith's daughters.

19. "Bulletin from the Hollywood Front," New York Times, September 9, 1934, p. X3.

CHAPTER FOUR

TURNABOUT

Turnabout was published in September 1931 and sold relatively well, attracting mixed reviews. Most enthusiastic was the *Boston Transcript* (December 9, 1931), pronouncing that it contained "individual gems of highly sophisticated humor." Far less enthusiastic was the *Saturday Review of Literature* (December 5, 1931), which commented,

"It is a pity that the publishers have taken occasion to announce *Turnabout* on the wrapper as a book which Anatole France might have signed, for, of course, Anatole France's distinguished mark was wit, and there is no wit in *Turnabout*. But though it has not wit, it shows flashes of irony, and contains plenty of knockabout, none-too-delicately-seasoned fun, of the type which used to keep the audiences of the old unreformed music-hall stage in roars of laughter."

Expressing an opinion that might relate to many of Thorne Smith's novels, the reviewer in the *New York Times* (September 27, 1931) wrote that "Some of the situations are very funny, but many of them inspire only acute fits of melancholy. The trouble is that Mr. Smith does not know when to stop."

Unlike other Thorne Smith novels, *Turnabout* boasts an equally matched male-female couple in Sally and Tim Willows. They are a well-to-do suburban couple in their thirties, married for five years, and Tim has a good position in New York with the Nationwide Advertising Agency, Inc. The agency is by headed by Mr. Gibber, who is a true believer in the power of advertising, believing that Christianity "had been handicapped and its rapid spread retarded because the Nationwide Advertising Agency had not been in existence during the time of Christ."[1] Smith satirizes the agency and its head, as Mr. Gibber spends hour after hour pontificating on the need for brevity.

Turnabout opens with the couple preparing for bed. Tim is surprisingly nude except for a pair of socks, the slow removal of which infuriates

Sally. Several pages are devoted to the loss of the socks and Tim's wiggling of his toes. Sally is equally infuriated that Tim refuses to wear pajama bottoms; "Real men take their pajama trousers off when they go to bed," he tells her.[2]

Overlooking the constant bickering of the two and getting steadily annoyed with it is a small Egyptian statue known as Mr. Ram, a wedding present from Tim's uncle Dick Willows. Completing the household is Dopey, the dog, who we are advised "had few friends. He was also a snob."[3] Dopey takes a surprising amount of insults and physical blows from Tim, but never loses his love for the man, upon whom he fawns.

The plans for bed are interrupted by neighbors who come for what appears to be a wife swapping party. It is "Suburbia at play," as Tim comments.[4] The latter, who has struggled into a pair of pajamas, is "regarded with interest"[5] by the ladies in the room, and Sally is enthusiastically greeted by neighbor Carl Bentley, with whom she is perhaps having an affair. Tim, himself, is involved in an affair with divorcée Claire Meadows. Smith's attitude towards extramarital relations as practiced at wife swapping parties such as those suggested here is ambivalent. He writes,

"The festivities over, these fair ladies would be returned to their husbands a little bit thumbed and dog-eared and more than a little drunk. It was one of those sportive occasions at which enmities are inevitably aroused and sordid recriminations incubated, for by the very nature of things there are few husbands and wives whose limits of conduct and powers of self-control register exactly the same. One or the other half of the tandem is sure to go too far."[6]

When Tim finds Carl Bentley in the kitchen with his wife, he takes a rolling pin and hits him over the head. He and Sally assume Bentley is dead and bury him in a coal bin. It is the first of many humiliations that the poor Bentley will endure. Next morning, on the train into New York, Tim discovers Bentley is very much alive and a fellow passenger.

That night, Sally and Tim again argue, with the emphasis on the latter's socks and toes. When Tim announces he would rather sleep with Dopey, Mr. Ram says to himself, "That settles it…I'll have to take steps this very night."[7] Such steps involve Tim and Sally exchanging bodies. He becomes Mrs. and she becomes Mr. Willow. The change, of course, leads to a variety of farcical situations as each try to cope with matters of hygiene, the wearing of each other's clothing and a change in daily habit, with Sally's now going off to the office. It also leads to Sally's impregnating her husband — what might be considered the ultimate revenge of a woman upon a man. As the clerk at the hospital during the birth comments, "If men had to have babies there wouldn't be any sex life," which leads Sally to comment, "Perhaps Mr. Volstead would introduce an amendment for birth prohibition." The clerk responds, "It would be a damn sight more popular than his other one."[8]

In between the sex change and the birth, Sally must deal with a difficult client, Tom Burdock, which involves much consumption of alcohol and incarceration in a hospital morgue. Tim, as Sally, confronts Carl Bentley. The poor man is forced to strip down to his union suit and then paraded at gun point through the town with the rear open. "Unbutton you little trap door...I want everybody to see it flap," Bentley is told as he flashes his backside.

All ends relatively sanely after Tim as Sally has given birth. He has avoided alcohol during the pregnancy but continues to smoke his cigars. An advertising campaign by Sally, as Tim, for union suits with flaps that never flap proves a huge success. Uncle Dick writes that he will support both Tim and Sally in relative luxury for the rest of their lives. Mr. Ram reverses the sex change. "After all, was he not...a man at heart? Did he not entertain himself all of man's narrow prejudices against bearing children?" With Dopey to hand and watching over the newborn child, Sally and Tim embark for Europe.

The basic premise of *Turnabout*, physical transformation, is sound and entertaining, if not entirely original. A similar concept is to be found in Ovid's *Metamorphoses* and Apuleius' *The Golden Ass*. F. Anstey's *Vice Versa* has a father exchange bodies with his son, although, of course, there is nothing sexual in the transformation.[9] *Turnabout* provides for social commentary on the lack of understanding between men and women, with, it might be argued, Tim's experiencing a form of rape as Sally gets him pregnant. Man in the form of Tim learns what it is not to be the dominant, aggressive sex. What is at fault are the amount of extraneous situations.

Thorne Smith, well recognizing his own faults, was pleased with the end result. He wrote to Roland Young, "It is pleasantly pornographic and sweetly salacious. It fails utterly to make sense."[10] Smith sent a copy of the book to gossip columnist Louella Parsons, whose first name he managed to misspell. It is inscribed, "In spite of all evidence to the contrary I really have a clean mind — at times."[11]

Before *Turnabout* became a film, it was a play — or at least the "idea" within the novel became a play. A farce in three acts by Paul Harvey Fox and Benn W. Levy, *If I Were You* has a pixie-like Irish maid, fascinated by witchcraft, exchange the bodies of the couple for whom she works. The wife enjoys cigars, while the husband is now involved in dressmaking and thinking of imminent maternity. Fox produced and Levy directed, with his wife, Constance Cummings as Nellie Blunt and British actor Bernard Lee as Arthur Blunt, who was now a chemist rather than an advertising exectutive. Later known for his stalwart character parts, Lee must have been quite something as the effeminate, transformed husband. The troublemaking maid was played by Betty Field.

The play opened in Boston in January 1938, moved to Washington, D.C., and then opened at New York's Mansfield Theatre on January 24, 1938. It was not well received. In the *New York Times* (January 25, 1938), Brooks Atkinson wrote,

"Since Thorne Smith never resorted to subtleties in search of the guffaw, the author of *If I Were You* cannot be charged with debasing a comic idea. But it remains to be proved that his moonstruck improvisations can stand the glare of the footlights...Miss Cummings galumphs and bellows through the part of the masculinized Mrs. Blunt like an amateur tomboy with no sense of humor. Although that may be performing, it is not acting."

The actress, who enjoyed the challenge of being a man and the smell of cigars, noted that "Some [critics] thought the packed audiences were movie fans of mine. Others didn't relish the thought of me as a man; that the material was distasteful. But I'm glad I did it. It was a different role and called for me to extend my range which is always good."[12]

The anonymous critic in the *Los Angeles Times* (February 4, 1938) was far from sympathetic towards Cummings, noting she "has now reached that part of the lesson book which tells how to read lines." The reviewer was equally negative towards the play, describing it as an example of the war between men and women,

"But the authors see fit to do nothing at all with their idea except push it into the lives of a young chemist and his wife and ask the audience to devote the rest of the evening to watching the young couple push the idea out of their lives.

"Still, the farce, if farce it must be, could have been saved if it had been played with a wild whoosh, the actors whooping after each other all around the furniture and tearing the stage and audience loose from their senses. Benn Levy has elected to have the whole thing played deliberately, one word coming after another like the tick-tocks of a clock."

If I Were You closed after only eight performances, and has not been revived.

As with *Topper*, the screen rights to *Turnabout* were acquired by Hal Roach. Clare Booth Luce was initially signed to adapt the novel, but she was subsequently replaced by the little known trio of Mickell Novak, Berne Giler and John McClain, with additional dialogue provided by Rian James. Some years later, the film critic for the *Los Angeles Times* commented sarcastically that the distinction between a man becoming a woman and a woman becoming a man was hard to make in a community as sexually confused as Hollywood.[13]

The production was budgeted at $457,650.00, and began filming at Roach's Culver City studios on February 19, 1940. With a salary of $50,000.00 for five weeks work, Adolphe Menjou received star billing (but below the title), rather than Carole Landis and John Hubbard playing Sally and Tim Willows.

Turnabout reunites quite a few individuals earlier associated with Hal Roach's unsatisfactory, prehistoric drama, *One Million B.C.* As members of the Roach organization, cinematographer Norbert Brodine and special effects expert Roy Seawright were naturally active on both films. Mickell Novak is as little known as her fellow screenwriters on *Turanbout*, but, unlike them, she had made her first film contribution as a writer on *One Million B.C.*, worked on two other Hal Roach productions and ended her four film career with *Turnabout*. The daughter of silent screen star Jane Novak, Mikell Novak married producer Walter Seltzer in 1938, and died, at the age of ninety-one in Los Angeles in January 2009.

Carole Landis had previously starred for Hal Roach, opposite Victor Mature, in *One Million B.C.*. *Turnabout* certainly provides Landis with a stronger and better part. On screen since 1937, she had never been a major star, and ironically she received more publicity and fame after committing suicide in the summer of 1948 as a result of the breakup of her relationship with the married Rex Harrison.

John Hubbard has the look of a poor man's Robert Montgomery, although some critics have compared him to Franchot Tone. Whoever he has been equated with, he is quite definitely a poor substitute. He has a good physique, but neither the face nor the acting ability of a major star. Hubbard made his film debut with Cecil B. DeMille's *The Buccaneer* in 1938, and then went under contract to Hal Roach, playing the second male lead in *One Million B.C.* Military service in World War Two damaged his career, and on his return to films he was assigned only to "B" movies. He worked in television in the 1950s and 1960s, ended his film career with *Herbie Rides Again* in 1973, and moved on to selling cars in the San Fernando Valley area of Los Angeles. He died in November 1988 at the age of seventy-four.

As evidence of his name value, Thorne Smith also received star billing, with a separate credit card. Reporting that the film was about to start shooting, the *New York Times* (January 15, 1938) noted that when its production had been discussed some months previous, *Turnabout* had "been discarded as being censorable." But this is, surprisingly, something of an exaggeration.

The novel had first been submitted to the Production Code Administration in September 1934 when it was planned as a film for production at Fox by Buddy DeSylva. In a memorandum to the files, Joseph Breen noted, "Mr. DeSylva stated quite definitely that he would rid the story entirely of any sex or suggestiveness which the book has."[14]

Hal Roach submitted his script to the Production Code Administration in segments. The PCA began reading the script in February 1940 and found no major problems. The first significant complaint came on February 15, 1940, when Joseph Breen wrote to Mat O'Brien at the Hal Roach Studios, Inc., that "The characterization of Mr. Pingboom as a 'pansy' is absolutely unacceptable." On February 22, there was an objection to Pingboom's line, "Toodle-oo, Timsy," and again concern as to the "'pansy' flavor." On March 5, 1940, a more major concern was raised in regard to the ending which was deemed "unacceptable":

"The inescapable inference in the present ending is that, although the personalities of your two leads have been switched back, their sex organs have become mixed up, and therefore the man is going to bear the child. Even in a fantastic comedy, we believe that this suggestion is definitely offensive, and hence not acceptable under the requirements of the Production Code."

On March 7, 1940, Hal Roach agreed to submit the ending for review prior to a preview or public screening of the film. On May 5, 1940, certificate number 6174 was assigned to the production "with the understanding that the picture, to be put into general release, will be exactly as shown to Mr. Breen on April 11th, 1940." On April 16, 1940, the PCA noted that the "suggestion" in regard to the ending had been removed from the finished film which now concluded with the couple facing the statue of Mr. Ram and telling him, "You have made us so happy." However, while Roach had supposedly agreed to cuts in regard to the ending and to Mr. Pingboom's appearance, no changes were made. Ultimately, Roach's recalcitrance appears to have paid off in that *Turnabout* was approved for screening without cuts by all local censorship boards except those in Ohio and Chicago.

In fact, the only concession that Roach seems to have made to the PCA was to "bloop" the name "Timsy" on the negative and on all release prints. Subsequently, more than sixty years later, when Robert Gitt at the UCLA Film and Television Archive preserved the film, he removed the "blooping" tape and restored "Timsy" to the track.

While the story and basic premise remained the same, there were some changes. Tim Willows was no longer an employee in an advertising agency, but a partner in one, Mannings, Willows and Clare, along with Menjou and William Gargan. Unlike the sophistication and satire of the *Topper* film, here Hal Roach, who also directed, returned in part to his silent comedic roots, often emphasizing the silly and unsubtle. This is particularly apparent in two sequences. The first involves a baby bear that Tim has mistakenly brought home as a gift for Sally, thinking it to be a small dog. The carrying cases of the two animals are switched at the pet store. As the bear proceeds to wreak havoc, Donald Meek as butler Henry is sent in to capture it, which he does using a bird cage. While only three minutes long, the sketch is so labored as to seem at least ten minutes in length to the viewer. James Donaldson was the bear's trainer, and, incredibly, he was on the payroll from February 28 through March 6, returning to the studio for an additional day on March 15[15]. The second comic sequence is less irritating and involves the efforts of Menjou and Gargan to destroy a radio playing the theme song for Marlow Pineapple Juice.

The Willows have moved from the suburbs to New York, and have a staff consisting not only of Henry the butler, but also a maid for Mrs. Willows and a cook, played with great vigor and a few good lines by Marjorie Main. Dopey the dog makes it into the movie, and he is an extremely large animal, every bit as large as that envisaged by Thorne Smith. The novelist described Dopey as, "If not the largest of all animals at least the largest of all dogs,"[16] and Dopey on screen certainly fits that description. Tim Willows engages in assorted athletic activities, including jujitsu and an energetic massage, both at the office. The fast-paced entry of Tim into the office tends to emphasize the stilted, unnatural quality of the earlier scenes between him and Sally in the bedroom.

A typical start to the business day for Tim Willows (John Hubbard) in Turnabout, *as he talks on the telephone, dictates to his long-suffering secretary (Verree Teasdale) and receives a massage from Murray Alper.*

Aside from the Willows household and the advertising agency personnel, the viewer is introduced to the wives of Manning and Gargan, played by Mary Astor and Joyce Compton. They are first seen in the company of Sally setting out "to spend the boys' money." Also making an early appearance is Franklin Pangborn as Mr. Pingboom, or Ping Pong, as the reception refers to him. Tim Willows has no wish to see the prospective client, but Sally, in her husband's body, will easily win him over with a discussion of nylons. Franklin Pangborn is noted for his prissy, homosexual characterizations, and in *Turnabout*, he is provided with one of his best — even the character name "Pingboom" is positively rife with gay meaning.

The main client of the agency is Julian Marlowe, played by the always-impressive Berton Churchill. Sally, as Tim, manages to lose his account for the agency, but later, as herself, wins Marlowe and his company back. Initially, Roach planned to use real companies, and a beach scene shot at the agency was to be for Dole Pineapple Juice, with a mammoth can of the juice in the shot, with the trade name prominently displayed. Another client at the agency was to be Chesterfield Cigarettes. The Production Code Administration firmly objected to such obvious product placement, which, of itself would have been most unusual for a film of this period.

Instead, there is no clear indication as to the names of any products being advertised in the two visits to the studio, the second of which has Sally in her husband's body reacting with near-hysteria to the presence of two male models advertising underwear.

The novel takes only four chapters before the transformation takes place. The film takes a long, thirty-seven minutes. Sally is angered at the presence of Mr. Ram (played by George Renavent) in the bedroom. Tim explains that he has a "strange power" that can grant any wish, and, of course, the wish that Mr. Ram grants is that Sally and Tim change bodies. The change leads immediately to some effeminate humor as John Hubbard awakes in his wife's lingerie and swishes around the house and the office. Sally is suitably masculine, climbing a flagpole on the terrace of the apartment to put up an aerial, and revealing unflattering facts to the partner's wives that "she" had learned when still a "he."

Unlike the novel, the transformation lasts only one day. It is a day in which Tim, as Sally, learns from her doctor that she has been keeping secret from her husband the fact that she is pregnant. The Willows promise to behave and ask Mr. Ram to change them back. "This time for keeps." This leaves ten minutes of screen time to sort out various problems created as a result of the change. The bear escapes and is chased by Dopey, who is, in turn, chased by the bear. Obviously, the film should have ended with the Willows smiling gratefully at Mr. Ram, but, instead, Mr. Ram looks horrified, announces "I made a terrible mistake," and whispers something to Tim. "You mean that I...," says Tim. And Sally announces to the assembled company of Tim's partners, their wives, and Julian Marlowe that "Tim is going to have a baby."[17]

Hal Roach's *Topper* films had depended upon special effects. *Turnabout* had more to do with characterizations. The main title with *Turnabout* seen

in reverse and then moving to the correct position suggests a sophisticated production to follow, but, sadly, such is not the case.

Ultimately, *Turnabout* is a massive disappointment. It is not even a
grand failure, but a misadventure that should not have been allowed to
happen. Writing in *The New Yorker* (August 3, 1940), Russell Maloney

Turnabout: *Carole Landis and John Hubbard plead with George Renavent, as
Mr. Ram, for a return to normality.*

began by noting how much he had enjoyed the original story and that he
had "great hopes" for the movie version., but concluded, "*Turnabout* has
its funny moments, and its dull moments. The gags are mostly of the type
intended to 'build' with repetition; some of them do, some don't. When
they don't, it's awful. Nothing is more distressing than the sight of movie
comedians milking a laugh that isn't there." When the film opened at New
York's Roxy Theatre, Bosley Crowther was far from complimentary the
next day in the pages of the *New York Times* (July 27, 1940):

"This department maintained a stony silence…Call it a question of
taste. For, so far as we're concerned, this self-conscious fantasy of a husband and wife who reverse their biological status is a tired and tiresome
jape, as subtle as a five-cent stogie and just as aromatic. This is the sort of
joke that the boys chortle over at the annual 'smoker.'"

Writing in the *Los Angeles Times* (May 5, 1940), Philip K. Scheuer praised Hal Roach for "the courage of his convictions; the unorthodoxy, the unusual, the different do not scare him off. This is all to the cinema good," Scheuer continued, but "The trouble is that he does things either by halves (*Turnabout*) or doubly (*One Million B.C.*). I suggest that he appoint

Not even a star-studded supporting cast, with some of the best character players in the business, could help Turnabout: *surrounding John Hubbard, from left to right, are William Gargan, Adolphe Menjou, Mary Astor, Joyce Compton, Berton Churchill, and Donald Meek.*

an aide in the person of an official good-taster. For instance, such a good-taster might be able to tell Roach — and us — why the phenomenon of the husband speaking with his wife's voice is conducive to merriment, while that of the wife speaking with her husband's voice is distinctly unpleasant. He would also turn thumbs down on the tag shown at pre-view, in which logic (even the screwball logic of Author Thorne Smith) is tossed overboard for the sake of a laugh."

Even the trade paper *Daily Variety* (May 1, 1940) could find little about which to get enthusiastic. It advocated cutting the film by at least a reel and worried that the "swish characteristics" assumed by John Hubbard might cause offense outside of major metropolitan areas, and that "the sex implications…may or may not please general audiences." However, "The masculine attributes of Miss Landis will be taken as a matter of course."

The Hollywood Reporter (May 1, 1940) was equally unenthused, describing the film as "Somewhat uneven entertainment. It is funniest when dealing with situations directly from the book…The two routines with bear and dog should be dropped entirely." Only *The Film Daily* (May 7, 1940) was wholly enthusiastic, describing *Turnabout* as "a wild, wacky affair."

Turnabout received a star-studded premiere at Grauman's Chinese Theatre in Hollywood on April 30, 1940, serving also as a public preview and a press screening. As might be expected, Carole Landis and John Hubbard were there, along with Franklin Pangborn. The guest list was most impressive, and included Fred Astaire, Lucille Ball, George Burns and Gracie Allen, Charlie Chaplin, Bing Crosby, Alice Faye, Cary Grant, D.W. Griffith, Dorothy Lamour, Harold Lloyd, Louis B. Mayer, William Powell, Tyrone Power, Edward G. Robinson, Rosalind Russell, Norma Shearer, James Stewart, Robert Taylor, King Vidor, Hal Wallis, Jack L. Warner, Loretta Young, and Darryl F. Zanuck. Described as a "motion picture theatrical event" by the *Los Angeles Times* (May 1, 1940), the evening ended with a party at the Hal Roach residence.

Incredibly, *Turnabout* resurfaced in the summer of 1948 at a Saturday afternoon screening for youngsters at the Sunset Theater in Los Angeles. What the children made of the film is not recorded, although they probably enjoyed the sequence with the bear cub. A piece in the *Los Angeles Times* (August 31, 1948) advised parents and their children that "The exchanging of voices provides one of the most amusing effects, the dainty looking woman speaking in a rough bass and her spouse twittering in feminine manner. Finally when the 'he' learns 'he' is to have a baby, there's a pretty how-de-do!" Los Angeles parents must have had some explaining to their children after that screening, a situation with which I am sure Thorne Smith would have been delighted.

Turnabout returned as a television series in 1979, produced by Universal Television. It survived a mere two months, with John Schuck and Sharon Gless co-starring as a sportswriter and the vice-president of a cosmetics firm. The professional assignments changed, but there was still a Buddha-like figure. Of the first episode, directed by Richard Crenna, *Variety*

(January 31, 1979) complained, "Sexual double entendre was treated very gingerly on the opener, making somewhat bland a set of situations that cry out for a looser, raunchier approach."

Of course, the basic problem with a new adaptation of *Turnabout* either for screen or for stage is that since it was written in 1931, sexual mores have changed drastically. It is no longer outrageous for a man to dress as a woman or for a female to adopt a male stance. *Turnabout* was originally intended for a heterosexual readership. Today, the premise is not only a gay one, but also one that is heterosexual-friendly.

1. Turnabout in The Thorne Smith 3-Decker, p. 261.

2. Ibid, p. 216.

3. Ibid, p. 227.

4. Ibid, p. 240.

5. Ibid, p. 240

6. Ibid, p. 240.

7. Ibid, p. 273.

8. Ibid, p. 425.

9. With its plot involving a mother and daughter who change bodies, Mary Rodgers' 1972 novel Freaky Friday may be said to have its origins in both F. Anstey and Thorne Smith.

10. Quoted in Joseph Leo Blotner, Thorne Smith: A Study in Popular Fiction, p. 102.

11. This first edition of Turnabout is now in the author's collection.

12. Michael Roy Gartside, For All Seasons: The Story of Stage and Screen Star Constance Cummings, Bognor Regis: LaureMar, 1999, p. 130.

13. Philip K. Scheuer, "Battle Devil in Hollywood," Los Angeles Times, December 7, 1947, p. B1.

14. Memorandum dated September 6, 1934, Production Code Administration file on Turnabout, Margaret Herrick Library, Academy of Motion Picture Arts and Sciences. All other quoted correspondence comes from the same file.

15. Can it really have taken so many days to shoot the sequence? Yes, according to the Hal Roach production file on Turnabout at the Cinema Library of the University of Southern California.

16. Turnabout in The Thorne Smith 3-Decker, p. 226.

17. The concept of a man's giving birth is obviously intriguing. As recently as October 2009, the Woman Magazine of the British Sunday newspaper The Observer featured on its cover a nude male, "Mum" tattooed on his arm, with a baby apparently suckling at his breast.

CHAPTER FIVE

THREE ADULT NOVELS AND ONE FOR THE CHILDREN

Thorne Smith followed *Turnabout* with a children's novel, of which it was claimed by its editor at Doubleday, Doran that, like *Alice in Wonderland*, would also appeal to adults. Using a premise to which he would return with his last completed novel, *The Glorious Pool*, in *Lazy Bear Lane* Thorne Smith tells the story of Peter and Mary, who live in a square, uninteresting house, with no food, and at which even the field mice turn up their noses. Despite magic seeming to pass them and the house by, the couple had always believed in it, and so they are not surprised when Lazy Bear turns up on their doorstep and starts them on the road back to youth again, to, as Peter says, "all the lovely old lost things — the things we used to know."[1] Two sad old people become gay (in the old-fashioned sense of the word) children, with the girl aged ten and the boy aged twelve.

It is spending a night sleeping in a haystack that brings about the change in age. There, in the haystack the children meet Mr. Budge, whose voice is heard in response to their insisting they will not budge. The next day, the children come across a small circus, consisting of a clown named Mr. Bingle, a young female rider named Floret and two lions, who are twin brothers, named Albert and Rudolph. Together, the group experiences various adventures, including Christmas in the city. Somewhat abruptly, the two lions take off for an adventure of their own, leaving the other characters in a sort of fairy-tale limbo. At the close, the group are back together again with Mr. Bingle and Floret getting married.

As with any fairy tale, or for that matter any story by Thorne Smith, there is neither rhyme nor reason to what takes place here. There are certainly strong elements of Lewis Carroll and *Alice in Wonderland*, particularly in the part of the story dealing with Mary's abandoned doll from childhood, who is named Queen Elizabeth. (In that the Duke of Windsor would have been expected at the time to become the next King of England, there was no reason to suspect there would have been a real Queen Elizabeth again.) Thorne Smith was obviously a fan of *Alice in Wonderland*, and in *Turnabout*, for example, he has Tim Willows comment how much he likes the book, and that "The world is not overkind. I much prefer Alice's."[2]

At times, the humor in *Lazy Bear Lane* is quite sophisticated. For example, Peter and Mary think about having supper. And that is what they do — think about it. Peter then makes a vegetable stew using illustrations from a catalogue. Queen Elizabeth makes all of the characters princes and princess, giving them the entire world, with the exception of Perth Amboy, certain sections of Brooklyn and the extreme tip of the North Pole.

Lazy Bear Lane contains fourteen verses, most attributed to Peter. Typical is the "Wedding Song," consisting of five verses, which begins,

Mr. Bingle, take your bride.
Sing it far and sing it wide.
You are now no longer single,
So be careful, Mr. Bingle.[3]

Early on, Lazy Bear has something to say to Peter about the lines in his poems not scanning, and "something amiss with the meter."[4]

The illustrations in *Lazy Bear Lane* are the work of George Shanks. The two-page illustration which appears on the front and end pages, with the lions taking to the air in a plane, to the astonishment of those on the ground, is somewhat similar in style to that of Herbert Roese. The other eleven illustrations, throughout the book, are not. They are quite enchanting and often heavy in detail, almost Victorian in quality.

The stories in *Lazy Bear Lane* had originally been told to Smith's own daughters, who were somewhat younger than the central characters here. In dedicating the book to June and Marion, Thorne Smith added, "Also for all other nippers who like slightly peculiar animals and people with just a touch of magic to help the author out of difficult situations." The age group for which the book is intended has never been confirmed. As Joseph Blotner has written,

"The central characters in the book are a boy of twelve and a girl of ten…Some of the nuances in the quarreling between the old woman and man at the beginning of the story...seem a bit too mature (not improper) for these age groups. Some of the descriptions too, although beautifully written, seem too advanced for these levels. On the other hand, the story in general is probably too immature for children past the ten year level. Aside from these criticisms the book should be entertaining for children between five and ten years old and even sufficiently charming to hold the attention of an occasional adult reader."[5]

Unfortunately for Smith, *Lazy Bear Lane* was not a success. It sold less than 3,000 copies, has never been reprinted, and is virtually impossible to locate with its original dust jacket.

THE BISHOP'S JAEGERS

Lazy Bear Lane was followed by *Topper Takes a Trip*. It, in turn, was followed by *The Bishop's Jaegers*, whose storyline centers around underwear and the lack of it. It is not the titular figure Bishop Waller and his underwear that predominate but rather Peter Duane Van Dyck, the wealthy owner of a New York coffee company, and the two pairs of drawers that he has mistakenly donned. While attempting to rectify the problem, he is interrupted by his secretary, Josephine Duval, who stalks him as he leaves the office heading for his fiancée Yolanda's home. There he strips off, takes a shower, and is interrupted in the nude by both Josephine and Little Arthur, a pickpocket. The three hide in a closet. Later, when asked by Yolanda what happened in the closet, Josephine responds, "The usual thing...He was naked as a coot, wasn't he? What else but the usual thing?"[6]

Then it is off to the New Jersey ferry for the assembled company. For no explicable reason, an unidentified individual fires a gun at the ferry, wounding Peter in the arm. He is assisted by Bishop Waller and by a former model named Aspirin Liz. After the ferry gets lost in the fog and nearly collides with an oceangoing liner, the group take to a small boat, only to come upon another boat full of nudists. Arriving at the nudist colony, which is run by a man named Jones, the proud owner of a duck named Havelock Ellis, there is a collective strip, except that the Bishop is permitted to keep his jaegers. Following the bedding of Peter by Josephine, Jones and Yolanda pair off together.

Young Jones is rather well described by Smith: "Even in his unclad state there was a sense of satanic polish about this person. In his eyes dwelt a dangerously amused light, and his agreeable-looking mouth seemed capable of uttering quite acceptably the most objectionable blasphemies."[7] What Jones does announce is a return to the animalism of the conventional life the group has abandoned, a season of forgetfulness, with reading limited to delightfully illustrated pornographic books. Along with Havelock Ellis and a pipe-smoking philosopher named Horace Sampson, the group decides to "escape." They strip a passing motorist, take a ride on a truck and are captured by the police at a Coney Island amusement park closed for the season. An appearance before Judge Wagger works out thanks to journalistic intervention, and the group retires to the Half-Moon Hotel and a set of drawers in an epilogue titled "A Farewell to Drawers." Peter and Josephine decide to strip and check out the bruises they have received. The final words in the novel are, "And in a little while Josephine and Peter were matching the various bruises they had collected during the sound and fury of their flight. They were almost like little children about it, but…not quite."[8]

Havelock Ellis was apparently a real duck, an inhabitant of Free Acres. A gossip item of the time had it that Smith considered bringing Havelock Ellis to Hollywood with him, but that "Hollywood life might be too stimulating."[9]

It is all fluff, light-hearted and very silly. Yes, there is substance, but irrelevant substance, a great many incidents without pertinence. The excitement is in the chase and the loss of clothing rather than the climax, spread over a period of time, with two couples consummating their unmarried relationships. Sadly, Thorne Smith seems to suggest that life in a nudist colony is as dull as life in a New York office. All that leisure activity seems positively boring. Life just goes on, but without clothes and, apparently, without much sex. Indeed, the *New York Times* (November 20, 1932) commented, "The book contains near its close, seriously uttered, the shrewdest criticism of nudism we have yet encountered: 'The benefits derived from mixed nudity are far outset by the mental agitation it entails.'"

The novel was enthusiastically received by both critics and the public. In terms of sales, almost one-and-a-half million, *The Bishop's Jaegers* surpassed those of *The Night of the Gods*, *Topper Takes a Trip* and *Turnabout*. Typical of critical response was the above-mentioned review in the *New York Times*:

"Told with the author's customary outpouring of Rabelaisian humor, the story's every page is bestrewn with wisecracks, innuendos, sly double-meanings. Play on words, with the naughty implication always in clearest view, here reaches the zenith of crude but sure-fire comedy without ever, miraculously, seeming to descend to the merely dirty and offensive… Obviously not for the prim, this book; but gorgeous entertainment for people owning a wee mite gamey sense of humor."

Inscribing a copy to his Doubleday, Doran editor Malcolm Johnson, Thorne Smith wrote, "If I keep writing books like this and you keep editing them whose mind is going to get the dirtier first!"

RAIN IN THE DOORWAY

The writing of *Rain in the Doorway* supposedly began prior to Smith's Hollywood visit and was completed after his return, but in view of its April 1933 publication by Doubleday, Doran, a month when Smith was still in Hollywood, this cannot be correct. In all probability, the manuscript was delivered to the publisher prior to the Hollywood trip and proof read while Smith was on the West Coast. As in other novels, there is more than a hint of the Marx Brothers here, with their 1941 film, *The Big Store*, set in a department store coming immediately to mind.

The novel begins, somewhat unpromisingly, on a rainy New York early evening, as thirty-eight-year-old Hector Owen mentally surveys his life, from a doorway in which he has taken shelter. His wife Lulu is having an affair and his chief work is as the "urban bailiff for a wealthy estate,"[10] answerable to a group of heirs, one of whom has mysteriously vanished and for whose disappearance Owen is blamed.

"Slowly the door behind him opened. There was no sound. An immaculately clad arm with a carefully starched cuff at the end of the dark sleeve drew nearer to the figure standing in the doorway. A strong, brown hand, its nails meticulously groomed, politely but firmly took hold of Mr. Owen and deftly withdrew him from public circulation."[11] When Lulu Owen arrives ten minutes later, all there is to show her husband had been there is a still smoldering cigarette.

Owen and the reader find themselves in a department store like no other. A crazy, hellzapoppin' like world, where customers are seldom right except when they steal and sales clerks are given a free hand. He meets a seductive sales assistant named Satin and the three partners in the store, who decide to elevate Owen to the same position. There is an incredible amount of irrelevant and ridiculous conversation. There is an equally incongruous banquet, which takes up thirty pages and two chapters. For reasons unclear, the group moves on to a hotel, where Owen beds Satin and the partners' wives. There is much amusement from the ladies when Owen explains that he is stripped to the buff. The question quickly arises as to what is a buff, do the ladies have one, and how cute Owen looks with his. How brilliantly does Thorne Smith take an innocuous word and imbue it casually with a double meaning.

The hotel is a typical Thorne Smith creation, where the rooms come with female companionship. As the desk clerk explains, "The hotel provides accommodations for certain members of our indigent female population while they in turn provide companionship for our male guests. We consider it an exceptionally sensible arrangement."[12]

After much frivolity in the hotel, there is an encounter with a dead sperm whale, followed by an appearance in the divorce court, where the partners attempt to rid themselves of their wives to whom, it is revealed, they are not married. Back to the department store, which promptly catches fire, resulting in Owen's leading Satin out of the building and back into the rain:

"For a moment the girl hesitated, and Mr. Owen was surprised to see a look of unsuspected tenderness creep into her eyes. Then he opened the door and followed Satin back into the rain. And as an 'L' train thundered overhead all that lay behind him seemed to flicker and die out dimly, but with desperate eagerness, he tried to recapture something, if only a little, of the past — the past behind the door. The other past was now his present."

The change in tempo at this point is both startling and appealing. It is as if Thorne Smith had suddenly discovered how to write well rather than as if he were creating a Marx Brothers film in Hollywood.

The novel concludes with Owen's finding his wife and one of the heirs he represents in his bedroom. As the reader might have well suspected, Satin is revealed to be the missing heir. The couple leaves for a new life together. "For Hector Owen's inhibitions had passed beyond recall."[13]

Even in the fantasies that he wrote, Thorne Smith produced stories that were more believable than *Rain in the Doorway*. There are many typical Thorne Smith elements here — the unhappily married man, nudity, a courtroom scene, and even an Irish cop — but they do not gel as they have in other novels. And yet, *Rain in the Doorway* was just as popular as earlier novels with readers and reviewers. In the *New York Herald Tribune Books* (April 16, 1933), George Conrad, obviously influenced by the presence of the sperm whale, wrote "Mr. Smith's book might have been called *Moby Dick for Men*. There are moments when the fun is spun out into too much talk, but the narrative portions have a brisk and saucy ingenuity and the prevailing winds are laugh-laden."

A note of general caution was sounded by Paul Jordan-Smith in the *Los Angeles Times* (April 23, 1933); "Thorne Smith is one of America's most brilliant humorists. Indeed, I am inclined to say that he is the most consistently amusing of the lot. He is a man to treasure; a man to watch. But if I were his publisher I should advise him to publish less; not to produce a book more often than once in two years; and then — were I his publisher — should ask the editorial privilege of cutting most of his books exactly in half. Even the best humor cannot maintain a high level too long." Jordan-Smith then ruins his argument by concluding, "That would be my advice to one of my favorite authors; though in the case of *Rain in the Doorway* that advice is not needed."

SKIN AND BONES

Thorne Smith began writing *Skin and Bones*, or at least making notes for it, while working in Hollywood. He finished the book in the summer of 1934 at Free Acres, before returning to New York for the winter. For the first time, he and his family had sufficient funds to rent a larger apartment, suite 602-A at the Madison Square Hotel. According to Joseph Blotner, the suite consisted of a living room, two bedrooms, a bathroom, and a kitchenette. Smith was also able to hire a governess for his daughters.[14] The peripatetic Smith family did not stay long at the Madison Square Hotel, moving early the following year to 60 West 10th Street and then 215 West 13th Street. *Skin and Bones* was announced for publication in December 1934, but apparently delayed into early 1935. Despite being terrified of being heard live on radio, Smith agreed to promote the book on a radio program sponsored by Macy's Department Store, which at that time boasted of the largest bookstore in the world. Difficult as it is to believe, Thorne Smith is generally described as having been somewhat shy, a trait that is not apparent in his writing.

One wonders if Smith used the radio program to recycle some comments he has his hero Hector Owen make in *Rain in the Doorway* upon seeing the book department of the featured store:

"All the books in the world seemed to have been gathered into that department. He found himself unwilling to open the cover of even one of them. He thought of giant forests denuded for the sake of these books;

of millions of publishers and editors crushed beneath the weight of their spring and fall lists, of numberless bookstore owners resorting to theft and murder or else going mad in their efforts to keep from sinking in seas of bankruptcy beneath the steadily rising tide of current fiction. He thought of haggard-eyed book reviewers turning their bitter faces to those strange and awful gods to which book reviewers are forced to turn in the affliction of their tortured brains. He heard these abandoned men calling in loud voices for a momentary recession, at least, of the soul-rotting flood of books. He even thought of authors, and his heart was filled with indignation against that indefatigable ever hopeful tribe of word vendors. If it wasn't for the diligence of authors so many hearts would remain intact and so many hopes unblighted. Mr. Owen decided it would be better not to think of authors. No good would ever come of it."

Despite its title, *Skin and Bones* has most to do with the latter as Quintus Bland, a lanky, thirty-seven-year-old head of a photographic studio in New York, takes to turning into a skeleton on a regular but unpredictable basis after "inhaling the potent fumes of a secret chemical fluid with which he had been experimenting."[15]

Bland and his wife Lorna are not a happy couple. The maid Fanny is attracted to him, while Lorna only finds Bland of sexual interest when she is unaware of his skeletal identity and he calls himself Senor Toledo. Smith does not explain exactly what, sexually-speaking, Bland and his wife might do together with the former in skeletal form. Through Lorna the reader is provided with a description of the household, beginning with Fanny, who is

"a misplaced harlot…but I've a yen for the wench. She's so refreshingly depraved she keeps me from growing stale. A respectable servant in this house would soon give notice. Cook drinks and steals and tells dirty stories. Whenever I get lonely I go out to the kitchen and she tells me a new one. She gets them from the iceman, the milkman, and such like. When she has stolen so much of our silver we can't set the table she gradually gives it back, or lends it to us for a while. Our occasional gardener is a self-confessed hophead. Sometimes his hands shake so violently he can dig and weed in half the time it would take a normal man. When he's full of snow he's no good at all. Spends his time leaping hedges and playing he's a butterfly."[16]

Skin and Bones follows Bland through a variety of silly escapades, during which, when he is not in skeletal form, he is naked, usually pursued by aggressive women or aggrieved men. In the course of his adventures, Bland meets Mr. Blutter, who is in advertising, "one of those exceedingly trying persons who believe that the more people you knew the better off you were." He also becomes intimately friendly with the Whittles, a married couple who live in a large and ostentatious uptown hotel. "About it there was no suggestion of home atmosphere. For this reason the Whittles liked it, never having been able to get through their heads what home life was."[17]

At the novel's conclusion, Mr. Blutter leads a mob of masked men — the Guardians of America — to kill Bland. "Their sick, egotistical conception of patriotism, morality, and civic virtue made them far more undesirable citizens than the relatively honest gangsters of Chicago and New York."[18] For the first, and last, time, Thorne Smith displays a social conscience, strongly criticizing the groups of masked, hooded individuals that had sprung up in the United States in the 1930s, preaching "Americanism" and every bit as vicious and as evil as the already-well established Ku Klux Klan. The most infamous of such pro-Fascist groups was the Black Legion, which, in May of the following year, was accused of the murder of a public employee in Detroit.

The Guardians succeed only in wounding Bland, who is taken to a hospital, where the effects of the photographic fluid wear off.

Paul Jordan-Smith in the *Los Angeles Times* (January 14, 1934) commented that "Thorne Smith is no modern Rabelais," but then continued, "He is an American Tristram Shandy, who dances with Puck on nights when the moon is full, very full." While Fanny Butcher in the Chicago *Daily Tribune* (December 30, 1933) wrote that "The reader reels with amazement and laughter through 306 hilarious but utterly mad pages," there was the suggestion from others that perhaps Smith's novels were becoming formulaic and obvious. "Mr. Smith rather bores me," wrote the critic in the *Saturday Review of Literature* (January 6, 1934). "There is no doubt that a certain amount of him was funny, but I am completely sated with his books." He continued, paying tribute to the work of Herbert Roese, "Mr. Smith has a fertile fancy and is undoubtedly a sex-simulant. His books are enormously popular with the country-clubber. He has made the naughty-naughty school pay and pay well. Personally, I think his illustrator also deserves a great deal of credit. He can make young ladies with hardly any clothes on so extremely luscious."

The *New York Times* (December 31, 1933) commented,

"Mr. Smith maintains such a high level of ingenuity in these fantastic plots of his that it seems ungrateful to quarrel with *Skin and Bones*.

Nevertheless, there are signs in it that Mr. Smith has begun to reduce his humorous inventions to a convenient formula, and that in doing so he has lost something of the spontaneity and the irrepressible wit which made *The Stray Lamb*, for instance, so delightful."

In 1962, the legendary special effects expert Ray Harryhausen read the novel, at the suggestion of his wife. In his opinion, "it would make a very unusual, if eccentric comedy, which would have required careful handling by the proper writer and director."[19] Harryhausen made one key drawing of Quintus Bland in skeletal form rising out of his bed. Columbia Pictures was approached with the idea, but, ultimately, rejected the project as uncommercial. Harryhausen returned to *Skin and Bones* in the mid 1980s, but by this time had to admit that it seemed "unsuitable for more discerning audiences."[20]

Uneven as these four novels are, they are remarkable in terms of their variant storylines and the speed and efficiency which the author demonstrated in their creation. Four novels in a period of two years — 1931 through 1933 — is most impressive.

1. Lazy Bear Lane, p. 34.

2. Turnabout in The Thorne Smith 3-Decker, p. 250.

3. Ibid, p. 239.

4. Ibid, p. 30.

5. Joseph Leo Blotner, Thorne Smith: A Study in Popular Fiction, p. 58.

6. The Bishop's Jaegers, p. 109.

7. Ibid, p. 211.

8. Ibid, p. 311.

9. "Gossip of the Book World," Los Angeles Times, December 25, 1932, p. B8.

10. Rain in the Doorway in The Thorne Smith 3-Decker, p. 446.

11. Ibid, p. 462.

12. Ibid, p. 583.

13. Ibid, p. 698.

14. Joseph Leo Blotner, Thorne Smith: A Study in Popular Fiction, p. 38.

15. Skin and Bones, p. 2.

16. Ibid, p. 176.

17. Ibid, p. 239.

18. Ibid, p. 293.

19. Ray Harryhausen and Tony Dalton, Ray Harryhausen: An Animated Life, p. 293.

20. Ibid.

CHAPTER SIX

THE WRITER GOES TO HOLLYWOOD

While all the screen adaptations of Thorne Smith's novels were released after the writer's death, like so many of his contemporaries, he did make the trip to Hollywood, pleased with the easy money that screenwriting offered. Buoyed by the reported increased sales of all of his books in the past twelve months,[1] Smith joined the writing staff at Metro-Goldwyn-Mayer in November 1932.[2] He already had at least two very entertaining friends in Hollywood, comedy actor Roland Young and legendary star of stage and screen John Barrymore.

In an undated letter to Young, Smith wrote, "Tomorrow the four Smiths depart for Hollywood — or Chicago — on the Century…If you notice undue excitement in the Metro-Goldwyn-Mayer camp it's me. God only knows what it's all about and why. All I know is that I'm scared blue and feel strangely uprooted…Probably I won't last more than three months, but at that, if I behave myself I can't lose."[3]

THE PASSIONATE BUFF

The writer's Hollywood visit evinced minor interest from the press, with commentary from gossip columnist Grace Kingsley. Initially, she reported that Smith was adapting *Turnabout*, but, in reality, his first assignment at MGM was titled *The Passionate Buff* and intended as a vehicle for comedian Ed Wynn. A highly popular comedian in the *Ziegfeld Follies*, where he was billed as "The Perfect Fool," on the Broadway stage and on radio in the 1930s, where he was the Texaco Fire Chief, Ed Wynn (1886-1966) would later be nominated for an Academy Award for his very serious performance as Mr. Dussell, the dentist who takes refuge with the Frank family, in *The Diary of Anne Frank*.

The film was never produced and never got beyond a fifty-seven page treatment by Smith. Dated March 10, 1933, it emphasizes the often-frenzied nature of an Ed Wynn performance, as well as his radio persona as the Texaco Fire Chief, and is obviously tailor-made for the comedian. The treatment contains many typical Thorne Smith elements and plot contrivances.

Ed Wynn, the original Mr. T. Wallace Wooly.

Ed Wynn is Mr. T. Wallace Wooly, often given to hysteria, despite which he is fifth assistant auditor to the second assistant auditor in a large insurance company. "And nothing made Mr. Wooly more hysterical than the sound of the sirens of the fire engines. The man was a natural born Buff. He attended fires, he dreamed of fires, and fervently hoped for fires." He is also an inventor, summoning his inkstand from a hidden recess, for example. Wooly's only friend in the office is Miss Betty Jackson, "a well favored wench."

Hearing the sound of sirens and bells, Wooly leaves the office in pursuit of the fire. On his way, he comes across "a very funny looking dog," and contemplates setting it alight. "We could have a dog and a fire, too," writes Thorne, attracted to two favorite subjects. Upon return to his office, Wooly learns that he has been fired.

At this point, the viewer learns that Wooly had a grandfather James who was a fire chief, along with five children and a dead wife. The family, which also includes a horse named James (not to be confused with the grandfather named James), indulges in its nightly game of Fire Chief, but is interrupted by the sound of fire sirens. Going outside, Wooly is mistaken for a fireman and rescues the inhabitants of a burning house. Among the group is a beautiful woman in "scanty attire." Wooly's trousers catch on fire and he is persuaded to remove them, revealing long striped underwear. In typical Smith fashion, the woman responds to the revelation, "If you don't take them off, I'll drag them off for you."

Wooly's actions lead to his becoming a regular fireman at Fire House 23. There he is spotted by Miss Jackson, "who was passing along the street either by accident or design." Wooly takes her home to meet his children.

A week later, "having nothing better to do," Betty Jackson sets a small fire in her apartment. Using the new parachute that he has invented to help firemen leap from burning buildings, with victims in their arms, Wooly lands in Miss Jackson's apartment on the bed upon which she happens to be lying. "I was never so glad to get into bed in my life," says Wooly. "What a break." "Thank you," answers Miss Jackson demurely. "After this, you'll have to marry me."

As a vehicle for Ed Wynn, *The Passionate Buff* is not a bad concept. The problem is with its suggestive dialogue and equally raunchy situations. It could never have been approved by Hollywood's self-censoring Production Code Administration. And it is doubtful that the studio would even have considered putting it into pre-production.

Metro-Goldwyn-Mayer did release an Ed Wynn vehicle in November 1933, titled *The Chief.* There are minor similarities to the Thorne Smith treatment in that, of course because of his radio persona, Ed Wynn has a connection to the fire department — here he is the honorary chief of the Bowery Fire Department — and he does rescue a woman from a fire. None of the character names are the same as those in the Thorne Smith treatment, and the only clue that the writers of *The Chief* — Arthur Caesar and Robert E. Hopkins — might have read it is that their script gives the central character a genuine fire chief and hero as a father, just as Wooly had a grandfather who was a fire chief. There the resemblance ends. The story is set in the 1890s and primarily concerns itself with crooked politics.

WHAT A LIAR OR OH WHAT A LIAR

Thorne Smith's second project for MGM survives as a four-page "Narrative Structure," dated March 20, 1933, and a five-page "Story Treatment," dated March 29, 1933, and intended as a vehicle for another radio personality, Jack Pearl. A dialect comedian, Jack Pearl (1894-1982) was never as prominent or as important in entertainment history as Ed Wynn. Pearl was best known for the character of Baron von Munchhausen and the catchphrase, "Vas you dere, Sharlie?" The title for the project varies slightly, with the earlier work titled *What a Liar* and the later treatment titled *Oh What a Liar.*

Despite its short length, the Narrative Structure is far-ranging. It begins in Paris with the "real Baron" and his servant, Jack Pearl, heading by taxi for Le Bourget Airport, having missed the last boat train connecting with a transatlantic liner. "The picture opens at a furious note of speed which is maintained for some time," writes Smith. At Le Bourget, the two men strap on parachutes and board a charter plane. Over the Atlantic, both parachute from the plane, planning to land on the liner that they had missed, the *S.S. Digestic.* Pearl descends and falls into the arms of a beautiful woman, but the Baron plunges into the Atlantic and is rescued by the crew of a tramp steamer, on which he is forced to remain for the next three weeks. Because he has possession of the Baron's wallet and passport, Pearl is mistaken for his employer. "He is photographed, autographed and lionized."

After landing in New York, Pearl is hailed by the media and comes to the attention of Jimmy Durante in the role of a gangster. He has been told by a dying Chinese of a cave in the Gobi desert, filled with treasure, and decides to force Pearl to lead an expedition there. A second gang is headed by Polly Moran, whose lieutenant Thorne Smith hopes might be W.C. Fields, and she also learns of the treasure trove. Durante persuades Pearl to lead the expedition, and the two rival gangs arrive in China, where there is a musical number and a dance routine and an encounter with a gorilla named King Pong. After discovering the treasure trove, the two gangs are captured by local bandits and tied to stakes prior to being burned alive.

In the nick of time, the real Baron arrives, leaves with the treasure and fails to release the captives. King Pong arrives next and begins to undress Polly Moran, but she is wearing so many layers of clothing that he become tired and gives up. As a parody of the scene in *King Kong* in which the ape undresses leading lady Fay Wray, this notion is actually rather amusing. Pong leads the group back to civilization, and the final shot is of him with the four leaders, Pearl, Durante, Moran, and Fields, on his shoulders.

It is a complex, insane storyline, to which the brief summation fails to give full reign. Obviously, Thorne Smith has little regard for cost in terms of the locations and the hiring of W.C. Fields in what is a supporting role. He further suggests a Walt Disney animated sequence, "for which I have some rough ideas," to be added during the shipboard sequence, which is also to include "a hot routine" from a group of chorus girls.

Smith's treatment, which does not seem to connect to the earlier Narrative Structure, consists of little more than dialogue between Jack Pearl and a group of reporters. The comedian is first seen emerging from a taxicab on Park Avenue. "The crowd gasps when it sees the length of the immense beard flowing from his chin back into the recesses of the cab." Pearl enters a hotel lobby, and the scene — and the treatment — concludes with the elevator door closing on him. There is no discernible plot or storyline, and the only (relatively) amusing comedy line has Pearl commenting, "A lobby full of white women. What a sight for sore hands."[4]

At one point, it looked very much as if the film, as written by Smith, would actually go into production. On April 12, 1933, the *Los Angeles Examiner* announced that that for the first time Walt Disney would be loaning out Mickey Mouse to M-G-M for a film tentatively titled *The Experiences of the Biggest Liar*. David O. Selznick would produce and Sam

Wood was to direct the film, co-starring Jimmy Durante and Jack Pearl. Herman J. Mankiewicz and Thorne Smith are credited as the authors of "the original comedy."

The film for which Smith provided the storyline and treatment was, in fact, made, and released in October 1933 by Metro-Goldwyn-Mayer as *Meet the Baron*. Six individuals are credited for the script, storyline and dialogue, including Herman J. Mankiewicz, but Thorne Smith is not among their number. Walter Lang directs and David O. Selznick produces. Jack Pearl stars, along with Jimmy Durante, but Polly Moran is replaced by ZaSu Pitts, and W.C. Fields is not present. There is no contribution from Walt Disney. The story of *Meet the Baron* bears no resemblance to the Thorne Smith narrative, except that Jack Pearl does pretend to be Baron Munchhausen.

MENU

The only film originating from Smith's Hollywood sojourn for which he received credit is the short subject, *Menu*, released by Metro-Goldwyn-Mayer as the third entry in its short-lived "Oddities" series on September 23, 1933.[5] Shot in two-color Technicolor, *Menu* was directed by Nick Grinde, who had been active since the late 1920s, generally directing low-budget "B" pictures The ten-minute short is narrated by Pete Smith, best remembered for the "Pete Smith Specialty" shorts at Metro-Goldwyn-Mayer, of which this is not one. The Pete Smith shorts are generally shot silent with commentary by Smith covering the action. In that Thorne Smith's credit is for the story alone, it may well be that the narrator actually wrote the commentary. If such is the case, it is difficult to comprehend why Smith bothered to contribute a story that is nothing more than a lesson in how to stuff and cook a duck and how to bake an apple.

Menu opens with a shot of John Xavier Omsk, played by Franklin Pangborn, sitting at his desk and taking a drink of bicarbonate of soda to offset the problems caused by his wife's cooking. The action cuts to the family kitchen, where Mrs. Omsk, played by Una Merkel, is trying to stuff a duck. Unlike most players in a Pete Smith short, Una Merkel is actually allowed a line of dialogue. To help Mrs. Omsk, Pete Smith conjures up a professional chef, played by Luis Alberni. "Does he shake a mean nutmeg," we are told. The chef rejects the initial duck for a plump and fresh one, and the short quickly becomes a cooking demonstration, in which it is very obvious that the hands expertly dicing vegetables are not those of Luis Alberni. The short ends with a shot of Franklin Pangborn's jacket pocket and a hand disposing of the bicarbonate of soda, which again, suspiciously, suggests that a body double was used.

Despite is general lackluster appeal, *Menu* was one of three films nominated for Best Short Subject — Novelty at the sixth (1932-1933) Academy Awards presentation. It lost out to *Krakatoa*.

Also while in Los Angeles, Thorne Smith found time — on April 17, 1933 — to sign copies of *Rain in the Doorway* at the J.W. Robinson department store in the downtown area of the city. He was billed as the "American Rabelais" and the "maddest wag in bookdom." Three years later, in March 1936, as part of its fifty-third anniversary sale, J.W. Robinson was promoting a six-volume set of Thorne Smith novels for nine dollars.[6] Smith also appeared at a luncheon, hosted by Mrs. Jack Vallely, on May 1, 1933. One of a regular series on books and world events, the luncheon took place at the Hollywood Athletic Club, with Smith's fellow guests including William S. Hart. Three weeks later, on May 20, 1933, Thorne Smith left the city for New York on the ocean liner, the *Santa Cecilia*. On board ship, it is reported that Smith took part in a contest which required male passengers to sprint from one end of the boat to the other, carrying a suitcase. At the far end, the contestants opened the suitcase, donned the female clothing therein and raced back to the other end of the ship.

While the *Santa Cecilia* was negotiating the Panama Canal, Smith conceived of the idea for a story of a group of individuals lost in the jungle. He even came up with a title *Casuals of the Jungle*, but never worked again on the project.

Thorne Smith did consider writing a novel to be called *Innocence in Hollywood*, but nothing came of that idea. In reality, he appears to have cared little for Hollywood or the experience of being there. As he told Roland Young,

"I thought a lot more about Hollywood than Hollywood thought about me, Mr. Young. I still carry the scars. They did everything to me out there but take me for a ride, and the reason they didn't do that was because they kept cutting my salary so that I wasn't worth the price of gasoline. It got so bad that I thought they were going to ask me to pay to get on the lot."[7]

1. The Night Life of the Gods was in its ninth printing, Turnabout was in its tenth printing, and The Bishop's Jaegers was in its seventh printing, according to the New York Times, December 16, 1932, p. 22.

2. "Book Notes," New York Times, November 23, 1932, p. 17.

3. Quoted in ibid, p. 36.

4. Both Thorne Smith pieces may be found in the M-G-M Collection in the Cinema Library of the University of Southern California. There is also a copy of the treatment in the M-G-M Collection in the Margaret Herrick Library of the Academy of Motion Picture Arts and Sciences.

5. I am using the release date appearing In the trade paper Harrison's Reports; another trade paper, Motion Picture Herald, gives a release date of August 26, 1933.

6. The novels were The Bishop's Jaegers, Rain in the Doorway, Turnabout, The Night Life of the Gods, Topper, and The Stray Lamb.

7. Roland Young and Thorne Smith among Others, Thorne Smith: His Life and Times, p. 20.

Thorne Smith with his daughters, Marion and June.

CHAPTER SEVEN

NOT AN END BUT A LASTING LEGACY

Thorne Smith's death was sudden and unexpected. On June 21, 1934, while he, his wife and two daughters were vacationing in Sarasota, Florida, the novelist suffered a heart attack and died. He had been taking a late-morning nap, following a swim in the ocean, and was found by wife Celia when she came to tell him that lunch was ready. The body was shipped back to New York, and services held on June 27, 1934, at Campbell's Funeral Church, located at Broadway and 66th Street. Burial took place at Mount Olivet Cemetery on Long Island. Smith had so little faith in the future earnings of his books, wrote H. Allen Smith, that he neglected to write a will. Smith remembered him as "the kindliest of men. He loved dogs and cats and children. His conversation was brilliant, for he was a man of excellent education, acute perception, and flaring imagination. When he talked, whether in casual chitchat or in telling a story, his conversation carried much of the sharp flavor that went into his writing."[1]

Smith had a $30,000.00 life insurance policy, on which he been carefully making payments. Tragically, a few weeks prior to his death, he allowed the policy to lapse.

As Smith himself presciently writes at the conclusion of *Thorne Smith: His Life and Times*, "The words have at last been written. I come to an abrupt end."[2] He had told Roland Young that if his books had any meaning, it was to be found in the last paragraph of *The Night Life of the Gods:*

"Yet through the deep silence of the vast hall something of them seemed to linger — Meg's last little sigh still floated like a mocking kiss on the cold cheek of convention."[3]

Joseph Botner is of the opinion that the most self-revealing lines written by Thorne Smith are those that end his poem, "The Rhyme of the Lost Romance," published in *Haunts and By-Paths*:

...There is none who believes
The things I say were ever really true.
It would be nice, I think, and so do you,
To find the haunts a vagrant fancy weaves.
Alone is man at best, and bound to earth,
And so in solitude his soul conceives
Such idle tales, knowing their fragile worth.

I am inclined to be be less pretentious, and quote simply one of the last spoken remarks by the title character in *Topper*. "It was a fine party."[4]

THE GLORIOUS POOL

In its obituary, the *New York Times* (June 22, 1934), reported that a month earlier, Smith had written his publishers, Doubleday, Doran, that he was acquiring "the color of a burnt crow," and, at the same time, sent the manuscript of what was to be his last book, for which he was to have sole credit, *The Glorious Pool*.[5] In reality, *The Glorious Pool* was not completed. Doubleday, Doran assigned Robert Hunt to write the last seven chapters of the novel, working closely with Smith's wife and using the author's notes.

The Glorious Pool takes place over one night, and centers around sixty-year-old Rex Prebble and his equally old mistress, Spray Summers, whom he describes as "my antiquated troll."[6] Completing the household is the Japanese houseboy Nockashima (variously referred to as the "Jap" or, incorrectly, in that the fictional character was Chinese, as "Fu Manchu"), an aged bloodhound named Mr. Henry, who has lost his sense of smell, and Fifi, a French maid. The last has little to do with the story, but what would a Thorne Smith novel be without a French maid named Fifi?

The garden is dominated by the statue of a naiad, acquired by Prebble and named "Baggage." "Baggage was a lush figure of a wench, the creation of vanished hands that either had known women too well or else had been deprived of them entirely."[7] As with the statues in *The Night Life of the Gods*, Baggage comes to life and, along with Prebble, wishes that he might be young again. The wish comes true when he and Spray swim in the pool, becoming not only twenty-five again but also happily nude. There is some comic humor in the manner of Laurel and Hardy as a neighbor Mr. Gibbs decides to set fire to his house, only to confuse his dwelling with that of another neighbor, Charlie, who kindly offers to set fire to his house himself.

The arrival of the fire brigade provides the central characters with the opportunity to steal a fire truck, aggravate their neighbors and the police and charge through Crown's Cosmopolitan Department Store. After helping themselves with clothing from the store manikins, and Nockashima's dressing in drag, the group returns home, meeting en route with two gangsters, irrelevant to the plot. As one contemporary critic noted, "if they needed all that outside assistance they shouldn't have bothered about the pool in the first place."[8]

Chapter XII, "Sue Returns," introduces Prebble's wife and his nephew, Kippie, who looks like a younger version of Prebble. Spray had seduced Prebble three months after his marriage to Sue, who is well aware of the relationship. Knowing that she suffers from corns, Sue has sent the outraged Spray an anniversary present of a large pair of carpet slippers. Not surprisingly, when the couple visits Spray's home, Kippie is mistaken for Rex and taken into the mistress's bed. Sue is persuaded by Baggage to enter the pool and be rejuvenated. Rex re-enters the pool to emerge as a baby with an adult voice and demands. He quickly grows into a young man as Sue and Spray argue over him. Baggage returns to her pedestal, while the novel ends somewhat abruptly with Rex's pondering the choice between his mistress and his wife. "What would he and Sue and Spray Summers do? The magic of the evening had not failed. Rex was not uneasy. Whatever might happen now, he was practically sure that it would be fun."[9]

"As ever, the pious reader must be prepared for shocks and improprieties," wrote Paul Jordan-Smith in the *Los Angeles Times* (January 13, 1935). "Thorne Smith never considered the feelings of Puritans." At the same time, Jordan-Smith was forced to admit, "His last book is by no means his best." The trade publication *Kirkus* commented that the novel "compares favorably enough with his later work, though it lacks the real humor and originality of the early ones...The book is so frankly bawdy that by its very lack of innuendo and double meaning, it fails to shock."[10]

The Glorious Pool was published by Doubleday, Doran in December 1934. That same month saw the American publication of another fantasy, one that has stood the test of time well and was to become a major Walt Disney motion picture, P.L. Travers' *Mary Poppins*.

Prior to his death, Thorne Smith had also completed a short story, "Birthday Present," to be published in *Redbook* magazine and signed a new ten-book contract with Doubleday, Doran. Smith also contemplated a return to "serious" writing with a novel about an elderly couple reflecting back on their lives — rather like an adult version of *Lazy Bear Lane*, it would appear.[11] Smith's productivity was far from close to coming to an end. As he wrote to Roland Young, "I have no end of bright ideas, all nice and dirty, and I only hope that God has just enough sense of humor left to spare me until I have been able to get them off my failing chest."[12]

NORMAN MATSON AND *THE PASSIONATE WITCH*

The Glorious Pool was not the only posthumous Thorne Smith novel. In July 1941, Doubleday, Doran published *The Passionate Witch*, based on notes and an outline found among Smith's effects and, supposedly, the treatment for *The Passionate Buff* that he had written while under contract to M-G-M early in 1933. Hired to bring the project to fruition was Norman Matson (1893-1965), who had authored a couple of other fantasy novels in the 1920s. His first book, *Flecker's Magic*, published by Boni and Liveright in 1926 and reprinted in 1959 as *Enchanted Beggar*, concerns an American art student in Paris who receives a wishing ring from a passing witch. His second, *Doctor Fogg*, published by Macmillan in 1929, concerns a beautiful naked blonde transmitted from another civilization by an inventor, whose wife conveniently dies with the appearance of the new female. Matson's choice as Thorne Smith's co-author, if that is the right term, certainly makes sense based on his literary antecedents, but there is no known explanation as to why Matson was selected.

Norman Matson was married for a short period of time to Pulitzer Prize-winning dramatist Susan Glaspell. Her biographer identifies Matson as openly anti-Semitic and an alcoholic. She further writes that after leaving Glaspell in 1932, he rarely published anything and had difficulty finishing any work.[13] Odd indeed that Matson should have finished the work of another.

The Passionate Witch was promoted as a new Thorne Smith novel. He is the author, with the secondary credit reading, "Completed by Norman Matson." As confirmation in a way that this is a Thorne Smith book, the drawings are by Herbert Roese. Certainly, the reader would have a hard time denying the Thorne Smith influence on the plotline and the seamless construction that denies a suggestion that the story was started by one and finished by another. As Charlotte Dean wrote in the *New York Times*

(August 3, 1941), "Mr. Matson has done a neat job of finishing the novel Thorne Smith left incomplete at his death. No one would ever know that any but the shaky Smith hand had set up these fantastic creatures and more incredible situations. There are no visible seams to indicate where welding or patching may have been done. The Smith fans can take this for a straight Smith.

The connection to *The Passionate Buff* is very slight. The hero has the same name, T. Wallace Wooly, with the "T" identified here as standing for Ten-Eyck. Wooly is now the head of the insurance company, with Betty Jackson as his secretary. In the proposed film, it is Betty Jackson, not a witch, who sets a fire, and it is Betty Jackson who is rescued by Wooly. But not here. In fact, it should be little surprise that *The Passionate Witch* is not based on *The Passionate Buff* in that the rights to the latter would be owned by M-G-M as Thorne Smith's employer.

T. Wallace Wooly lives in Warburton, and is the honorary vice-chief of its fire department. When a fire occurs at the Hotel Monroe, Wooly rushes to the scene and rescues the naked and very attractive Jennifer Broome, a rescue that is recorded in the local press. Wooly becomes besotted with the young lady who is, it transpires after their marriage, a singularly unpleasant witch. Jennifer is described as having "a great glory of lustrous dark hair and slanting eyes, half-closed, the pupils a clear yellow light in shadow, a mouth curved in a short, catlike smile, mirthless as a cat's, cruel and passionate, small teeth flashing in a smile of pure joy."[14] She bewitches secretary Betty Jackson making her capable of writing only backwards and subsequently burns down her home. She slashes the head off a rooster in protest perhaps at Wooly's vegetarian ideals, and drinks its blood.

Jennifer dies, less than halfway through the novel. She burns down the local church — a remarkably demonic act for a Thorne Smith character to perform — and, wearing a mink coat, she is killed by a stone cross falling from the roof of the church. It is all more suggestive of *The Omen* than of Thorne Smith. Wooly plans to bury her, as befits a witch, at the intersection of two roads and with a stake through her heart. His plans are thwarted, and Mrs. Wooly is buried, "normally and unstaked,"[15] in the family plot in Cloudy Lawn Cemetery.

Unfortunately, before she died, Jennifer had cast a spell on her husband, whereby he could hear everything that anyone else was thinking. It is a situation that is slowly driving him insane. After a scene in a ladies

Turkish bath, a police chase and a courtroom appearance, all of which are classic Thorne Smith, Wooly discovers that the spirit of Jennifer survives in his horse, Rummy. At the town's July 4th parade, Rummy attacks Betty Jackson's car. However, as she pursues her prey, Rummy falls into a ten-foot hole at an intersection. In the hole was a crowbar, which went straight through her heart. Six weeks later, Wooly and Betty Jackson are on board a steamer bound for Bermuda.

The Passionate Witch is more carefully written in terms of its plot than a typical Thorne Smith novel. It is also somewhat "dark" in that the character of Jennifer is never appealing to the reader, and, of course, her death is quite extraordinary. Never before had Thorne Smith demonstrated the least belief in the power of God to destroy evil. The critic in the *Springfield Republican* (July 27, 1941) noted, "Witch Jennifer in this last book is malignant, the first Thorne Smith character to be drawn from black magic, and although all ends well for her happy husband her vindictiveness at times casts an unaccustomed gloom over the story. It is indulging in fantasy to say that when Thorne Smith created Jennifer it was already later than he thought, but the fact remains that although his last book is an unexpected feast, there is a skeleton at it."

Other reviews were comparable to those that Thorne Smith had been receiving through the years. In *The New Republic* (August 25, 1941), Otis Ferguson wrote, "It is the kind of light reading that gets pretty heavy after a while, but not quite so funny as average Wodehouse but the same rapid intervention and feeling of deliberate effort." "It doesn't make sense," commented *The New Yorker* (July 26, 1941), "but Thorne Smith admirers probably won't care, in spite of an air of strain now and then."

The anonymous critic in the *Los Angeles Times* (August 3, 1940) noted that the situation was pure Thorne Smith. "But, alas, Thorne Smith did not live to complete the yarn and the flavor is not quite what it should be. Even so the thing has high spots of hilarity, and there's not a Thorne Smith fan or collector who will not wish to add this diverting story to his collection."

I MARRIED A WITCH

I Married a Witch, the screen version of *The Passionate Witch*, bears as much resemblance to the original as does that same original to *The Passionate Buff*. Yes, Veronica Lake is a sexy Jennifer, but opposite her is Fredric March, playing not T. Wallace Wooly but Wallace Wooley. Why this subtle change to his name? The film begins in 17th Century New England as Wooley's ancestor watches Jennifer and her father (played by Cecil Kellaway), both of whom he has accused of witchcraft, being burned at the stake. Jennifer curses Wooley and his ancestors to perpetual unhappiness in love, and, in the present, she comes back to life as

Fredric March and Veronica Lake as Wallace Wooley and Jennifer in I Married a Witch.

the modern-day Wooley is about to marry Estelle Masterson, played by Susan Hayward.

As in the novel, Wooley rescues a naked Jennifer from a burning hotel. She succeeds in seducing and marrying him, and uses her witchcraft to help him win the gubernatorial election. As Jennifer's father returns to corporeal form, he takes away his daughter's powers and she is returned to being a spirit. However, proving that love is stronger than witchcraft, she returns to life, traps her father in a bottle of rum, and settles down to married life with Wooley, eventually giving him two sons and a daughter. It seems dubious that Thorne Smith would have approved of such a happy, domestic ending.

Luckily Veronica Lake was under contract to Paramount, having just completed shooting *This Gun for Hire* for the studio. Fredric March liked the script, and he was signed by the studio while vacationing in New York on March 16, 1942.

There were some problems with the production in that the original

A bewitching Veronica Lake in I Married a Witch.

screenwriter Dalton Trumbo argued with the original producer Preston Sturges, who disagreed with the director, René Clair. The script is primarily the work of Robert Pirosh and Marc Connelly. Released in October 1942, *I Married a Witch* makes pleasant watching, thanks to the light touch of Frenchman René Clair, who was earlier responsible for such classics as *The Italian Straw Hat*, *Le Million* and *The Ghost Goes West*. His direction of the last, which preceded the screen version of *Topper* and is very much in the Thorne Smith tradition, makes Clair a natural for *I Married a Witch*. Roland Young was a great admirer of the director, and after appearing in his 1941 film, *The Flame of New Orleans* commented, "his inventive mind is inexhaustible."[16]

I Married a Witch was a Cinema Guild production, produced for Paramount release. However, because of over-production, in September 1942, that studio sold the distribution rights to this film and others to United Artists.[17]

"Old friends of Topper will immediately recognize the spirit and style," wrote Bosley Crowther in the *New York Times* (November 20, 1942), a day after the film's New York opening at the Capitol Theatre. Crowther also noted that "The strange and beautiful illusion that Veronica Lake is completely unreal is...quite charmingly nourished...The illusion is thoroughly disarming, and so is this whimsical film." Edwin Schallert in the *Los Angeles Times* (December 18, 1942) complained that the plot was "contrived," but agreed that "there is enough hearty laughter evoked by what happens to asure the picture of popularity." The trade paper *The Hollywood Reporter* (October 19, 1942) described *I Married a Witch* "as one of the most delightful adult comedy realizations of the supernatural ever to emerge from Hollywood." *Variety* (October 21, 1942) was less enthusiastic, describing the film as "generally tepid."

Plans were announced in 2003 by producers Tom Cruise and Jane Wagner for a remake, to be released by Columbia. Danny DeVito was to direct, and there were early reports, dating back to 1998, that Cruise's then-wife Nicole Kidman was to star. Kidman subsequently was announced for a film version of the television series *Bewitched*.

BATS IN THE BELFRY

At the close of *The Passionate Witch*, the author writes, "Good-by, Jennifer. Good-by, Rummy. We will not see you again!" In fact, two years later, Jennifer, Wooly and Betty Jackson, now the third Mrs. Wooly (the first had died prior to the start of *The Passionate Witch*) did all return in Norman Matson's *Bats in the Belfry*, published by Doubleday, Doran. The title comes from a comment that a bartender makes about Wooly.[18] "Bats in the Belfry" is an outmoded expression meaning that someone is crazy or insane; the belfry is at the top of the bell tower on a church, where bats live in darkness and isolation.[19]

Seven years have passed since Jennifer was buried, but she has begun communicating with Wooly, generally on the radio, asking that he come and dig her up. When she uses mental telepathy to start a run on Wooly's bank, he and his board of directors are forced into action — and the ex-wife is exhumed in perfect sexual and physical condition. She causes consternation in the community to the delight of the male population and the outrage of the female. When the situation appears beyond a satisfactory conclusion, Wooly dies of an embolism. Like Jennifer, he becomes a ghost but she realizes when enough is too much. At his funeral, Wooly is restored to life and to Betty, and Jennifer's body is restored to the grave.

Matson's style is quite definitely more ordered, and less out of control, than that of Smith. But his construction is not always as appealing, and, frankly, the breakup between the ghosts of Wooly and Jennifer is very difficult to follow or comprehend. Matson does have a nice touch with a couple of rhymes:

A hermaphrodite adult in Texas
Was dreadfully confused by his sexes.
Oh, what am I for?
The poor thing would roar
As he gazed his ambiguous nexus.[20]

And

When I was but a nipper,
No woman wore a zipper.
'Twas slower, thus, the seeking longer,
Yet on delay doth love grow stronger.[21]

A reviewer in the New York Times (May 9, 1943) summarized the novel succinctly with the opinion, "There is a lot of drinking and the bibulous wit that goes with it, and much ribald humor." However, most contemporary commentators were of the opinion that the book was not in the same league as a genuine Thorne Smith work. The New Yorker (May 8, 1943) described Bats in the Belfry as "A capering tale told with a dogged determination to be as funny as all get-out, which (so the publishers say) will delight the heart of Smithomaniacs. Smithomaniacs will kindly move over to the far corner." "If you liked The Passionate Witch you'll like Bats in the Belfry, and that's about all that can be said," commented the Springfield Republican (July 4, 1943). "Mr. Matson is not as good as Thorne Smith, but no one expects that he could be. In continuing the Thorne Smith tradition he has attempted a pretty big job, and while it must be said that he rattles around a bit in Thorne Smith's shoes he does do an adequate job with the kind of material left over from the master's palette."

A modern commentator, Brian Stableford, has noted that "there is a deeper-lying uncertainty about Matson's own attitude to the mythology of romance and the possibility of ever living happily after marriage. Whether his superficial purpose is comic or moralistic, there is a bitter undercurrent in all Matson's fantasy fiction which is cynically suspicious of the glamour possessed by lovely young women and back-handedly contemptuous of the dullness of not-so-lovely wives. In this respect the books may be a little more revealing than their author intended, or might have wished."[22]

The popularity of Thorne Smith's novels showed no sign of diminishing after his death. In 1936, 1938 and 1943, respectively, Doubleday, Doran reprinted nine of Smith's novels in three volumes which might perhaps loosely be described as trilogies: *The Thorne Smith 3-Decker*, *The Thorne Smith Triplets* and *The Thorne Smith Three-Bagger*. The first contained *The Stray Lamb*, *Turnabout* and *Rain in the Doorway*, with the second volume including *Topper Takes a Trip*, *The Night Life of the Gods* and *The Bishop's Jaegers*, and the third, *The Glorious Pool*, *Skin and Bones* and *Topper*.

The descriptive word for such "trilogies" at the time was "omnibus." It is a concept of which Thorne Smith makes considerable fun in *Rain in the Doorway*. An author in the book department of the featured store explains that "I hope to be an omnibus some day."[23] A sales assistant explains to a confused colleague,

"It's one of those quaint ideas that occasionally get the best of publishers. Whenever an author isn't good enough to have his old books bought individually and still isn't rotten enough to be taken off the list entirely they publish an omnibus volume of his stuff, and surprisingly few people ever buy it."[24]

Thorne Smith's wife, Celia, came briefly back into the news in March 1943, when she was severely burned and her clothing caught fire while she was removing a pot of water from the stove at the family's Free Acres home.

POCKET BOOKS

A major event in publishing history took place on June 19, 1939 when Robert F. de Graff published the first ten titles in the paperback "Pocket Book" series, priced at twenty-five cents each. Along with a handful of classics, James Hilton's *Lost Horizon*, Agatha Christie's *The Murder of Roger Ackroyd*, Felix Salten's *Bambi*, Thornton Wilder's *The Bridge of San*

Luis Rey, and Dorothy Parker's *Enough Rope*, there was Thorne Smith's *Topper*. It had truly become a classic of 20th Century literature. Pocket Books was later to publish other Thorne Smith titles: *The Stray Lamb*, *Did She Fall?*, *The Night Life of The Gods*, *Turnabout*, *The Bishop's Jaegers*, *Rain in the Doorway*, *Skin and Bones*, and *The Glorious Pool*.

By 1952, it was reported that he was one of the five most popular authors to be found in paperback editions, along with Erle Stanley Gardner, Erskine Caldwell, Ellery Queen, and Mickey Spillane.[25] By

The Pocket Books edition of Did She Fall? *emphasizes the name of the author and that the story is "a prankish mystery."*

the late 1950s, *The Passionate Witch*, first published by Pocket Books in 1946, had sold a reported 2,210,000 copies. It was surpassed in hardcover sales by two other Thorne Smith titles — *Topper* with sales of 2,560,806 copies and *The Glorious Pool* with sales of 2,572,945 copies.

The paperback editions may have sold initially for only twenty-five cents each, but that was only one eighth of the cost of an original hardcover edition. *Topper*, *Dream's End*, *The Stray Lamb*, *Did She Fall?*, *The Night Life of the Gods*, *Turnabout*, *Topper Takes a Trip*, *The Bishop's Jaegers*, *Rain in the Doorway*, *Skin and Bones*, *The Glorious Pool*, and *The Passionate*

Witch all were published at two dollars each. The trilogies were priced at between $2.50 and $3.00 apiece, but in 1943, they were being sold at drug stores for only $1.49 each. At the same time, cheap Sun Dial Press hardcover editions of individual Thorne Smith novels were selling at only seventy-nine cents each.[26]

The release of the trilogies and of the paperback editions may, in some part, be a reflection of the interest in Thorne Smith generated by the films based on his novels. A moviegoer viewing, say, *Night Life of the Gods*, could well have been influenced to purchase other Thorne Smith novels not as yet, or never to be, adapted for the motion picture. Certainly, the trilogies were well received by the critics. A reviewer for *Kirkus* noted that *The Thorne Smith 3-Decker* "Gives an opportunity for making new Thorne Smith fans — for reeducating those who know him in one vein and not in another. Good value for the money."[27] Upon publication of *The Thorne Smith Three-Bagger*, the *New York Times* (March 28, 1943) wrote, "Mr. Smith had a one track mind but the track is a common one, and he decorates it with a zaniness all his own, spicing the already spicy mixture of well shaped, amorous women and eternally ardent men with uncorporeal bodies."

Thorne Smith enjoyed considerable posthumous popularity in the United Kingdom. Originally published in London by Arthur Barker Ltd. in June 1938, *The Glorious Pool* was in its seventh edition when published by Methuen & Co. Ltd. in August 1939. By 1952, it had been reprinted a further sixteen times. *Did She Fall?* was first published in the U.K. by Arthur Barker Ltd. in October 1936. The fifth edition was published by Methuen & Co. Ltd. in November 1939. Methuen published the fourteenth edition in 1952.

In his prominent 1940 survey, *The American Novel*, Carl Van Doren wrote enthusiastically of Thorne Smith:

"...he had a distinctive talent and an engaging vein. His novels were all farce and fantasy, perpetual gay adventures in a fluid universe...Thorne Smith's favorite hero is a man who, settled largely by chance in a dull life, discovers that he has a capacity for pleasure and at once finds opportunities swarming round him. Most of the courting in the stories is done by women, swift, witty, irrepressible daughters of nature who regard men as slow-going creatures that need to be civilized by laughter and love. The books have no problems and no penalties, since the plots are cheerfully irresponsible. They would be shocking if they were not so funny. Though the world Thorne Smith created is not in the least real, it is not remote in time or place. With an instinct for nonsense he took the smart life of his own day and let it run wild and free in his novels."[28]

The Thorne Smith name remained familiar to readers. When *Time* magazine (August 7, 1950) noted the Spring 1951 publication of actor David Niven's first novel *Round and Rugged Rocks* (retitled *Once over Lightly* in the United States), it was described as having "a Thorne Smith touch."

In 1951, Joseph Blotner received a doctorate of philosophy from the University of Pennsylvania, submitting as his dissertation subject, *Thorne Smith: A Study in Popular Fiction*. Because Blotner had attended high school with Smith's daughters, he had unique access to family archives, and his dissertation stands as the definitive record of the novelist's life. As Blotner recalls, it was not easy persuading his dissertation committee to accept a thesis on such a frivolous subject as Thorne Smith. Luckily, dissertation director Robert E. Spiller not only approved the subject but also provided its subtitle. In old age, Blotner looked back at his commentary on Thorne Smith and comes to the conclusion that the novelist was "very gifted" and that, "I took a rather snide attitude towards him; I should have given him more credit."[29]

The advent of a new type of men's magazine, *Playboy*, in 1953 led to a surprising revival of interest in the novelist. *Playboy* published two "short stories" modified from two of Thorne Smith's novels. "The Boss's Breeches," adapted from *The Bishop's Jaegers* was published in the July 1954 issue of *Playboy*, and "The Advenures of Hector," taken from *Rain in the Doorway* appeared in the October 1955 issue.[30] Each short story was accompanied by a new introductory illustration, the first by Paul Pinson, and the second by Justin Wager. *Playboy* promoted both as being "racy" and both generated what was basically positive commentary from readers, at least as published in the magazine.

Credit for introducing Thorne Smith to *Playboy* readers probably belongs to Ray Russell (1924-1999), who was the magazine's associate editor from 1954-1955 and its executive editor from 1955-1960. Russell described his time at *Playboy* as a "delightful detour" from his writing career, which was devoted to short stories and novels with gothic and/or supernatural themes, which might have been, but are not, in the Thorne Smith tradition. Russell's best known work is the short story "Sardonicus," which he adapted for the screen in 1961 as *Mr. Sardonicus*. Stephen King described "Sardonicus" in the *New York Times* (March 22, 1999) as the "finest example of modern gothic ever written."

As late as March 1957, *Playboy* reviewed the Franco-Swedish film *La Sorcière* as being "Thorne Smith with a foreign accent." The film features Marina Vlady as a Swedish woman who is supposedly a witch, and the Thorne Smith connection might just as easily have been a Norman Matson connection.

While interest in Thorne Smith's novels continued into the 1950s, a decade later enthusiasm had waned. By the early 1960s, none of the writer's books were still in print. Could the political tenor of the times have had anything to do with Smith's falling out of favor? At least one academic believes so, although the argument is somewhat diminished in view of *Playboy*'s use of Thorne Smith humor. Howard Steven Jitomir writes that,

"In the 1950s, when Smith's novels went rapidly out of print, the United States was afflicted by an unreasoning fear of communist subversion from within the country and communist attack from without...The 1950s, in short, was not a time to criticize or laugh at anything which was American; and of all modern humorists, Smith is the most unrelenting and comprehensive in his attack on American society. He opposes the success ethic with such vigor that a nation under stress could only interpret his work as an attack on free enterprise. He mocks religion and morality in general and Christianity in particular, so he is obviously a godless soul attempting to pervert American values...He had ceased to be funny."[31]

It is an interesting, if not totally, convincing theory. Certainly, an argument might be made that Smith's novels are strongly anti-establishment. Rather like the early slapstick comedies were produced for lower class, immigrant audiences, who enjoyed seeing those in power being ridiculed, so did Thorne Smith's novels take on groups who could make one's life miserable, most prominently, the police and judges, both of which were the subject of often vitriolic ridicule. But then, there are always those in society who will object to fun, as Topper himself comments, "Fun fills the divorce courts and digs untimely graves."[32]

It was not until the 1980s that paperback publisher Ballantine Books reissued six of the novels: *Topper, Topper Takes a Trip, The Night Life of the Gods, The Stray Lamb, Turnabout*, and *Rain in the Doorway*. The last was promoted as a work of science fiction, a somewhat dubious claim.

In 1999, Random House's Modern Library reprinted three Thorne Smith titles in new paperback editions, with biographical and critical introductions. The first was *Topper*, published on February 2, 1999, followed by *Topper Takes a Trip* and *The Night Life of the Gods*, published on December 28 of the same year.

In the last twenty years, there would seem to have been a decline in interest in Thorne Smith's novels. His name is largely forgotten except among die-hard enthusiasts. At the same time, first editions of Thorne Smith's novels continue to sell, or are at least advertised for sale, by anti-quarian booksellers at high prices. As I write, Robert Dagg Rare Books in San Francisco has for sale first editions of a number of Thorne Smith's books, with their original dust jackets, at prices ranging from $250.00 for *The Glorious Pool*, through $450.00 for *Topper Takes a Trip*, to $950.00 for *The Night Life of the Gods*.

THE INFLUENCE OF THORNE SMITH'S WRITINGS ON LATER FILMS

As early as 1946, a comparison was made between the Bud Abbott and Lou Costello vehicle *The Time of Their Lives*, in which the latter played an earthbound ghost accompanied by a female companion, played by Marjo-rie Reynolds, and Thorne Smith's books. And there are certainly elements here from both *Topper* and *The Passionate Witch*.

In determining the extent to which Thorne Smith's writings have influ-enced more recent film and television productions, one must be careful not to over-exaggerate. There have been a vast number of films involving ghosts and ghostly situations, including for example *Ghostbusters* (1984) and *Dead Again* (1991), neither of which may be considered as represen-tative of the Thorne Smith legacy. To be in the Thorne Smith tradition, productions must be subversive rather than violent, should not take death seriously, should be comedic in as sophisticated a manner as possible, and non-sentimental. The last category lets out Frank Capra's *It's a Wonderful Life* (1946) with its overly emotional storyline.

Among those titles of which perhaps Thorne Smith would have approved are *Kiss Me Goodbye* (1982), starring Sally Field; *Made in Heaven* (1987); *All of Me* (1984), starring Steve Martin and Lily Tomlin; the Bill Cosby vehicle *Ghost Dad* (1990); *Ghosts Can't Do It* (1990), starring Bo Derek of whom I am sure Thorne Smith would have been most appreciative; and the British entry *Truly Madly Deeply* (1991). One of the most obvious titles to honor the Thorne Smith legacy is not American, but the Brazilian feature *Dona Flor and Her Two Husbands* (1978), in which the deceased, unreliable husband of Sonia Braga returns, in the nude, just as she has found a new mate. There was a 1982 American remake, *Kiss Me Goodbye*.

One academic has pointed out that, as with *Topper*, a character's "alcoholic delusions" makes literal "the link between ghosts and liquor as an alcoholic 'spirit,'" in a number of films, citing *Ghost Dad, Kiss Me Goodbye, Mr. Destiny, Alice, Almost an Angel, Maxie, All of Me*, and *Heart Condition*.[33]

An unusual "homage" to *Topper* and to Cary Grant is the 2004 Canadian film, *Touch of Pink*, in which the ghost of the actor is the guardian angel to a gay Canadian Muslim. Directed and written by Ian Iqbal Rashid, and starring Kyle MacLachlan as Grant, the film takes its title from the 1962 Cary Grant vehicle *That Touch of Mink*.

Topper's continuing appeal was also evident in at least one theatrical production. When Noel Coward's *Blithe Spirit* opened at London's Saville Theatre on April 17, 1940, the Thorne Smith influence was very obvious. Thanks to the somewhat eccentric efforts of Madam Arcati, the ghost of novelist Charles Condomine's first wife, Elvira, materializes, and she is as outrageous as Marion Kerby in *Topper*.[34] In its report on the London production, the *New York Times* (July 13, 1941) headline read, "Coward Pulls a Topper," while admitting later in the article that Coward's "touch is infinitely lighter than Smith's."[35]

It is worthy of note that as early as 1935, *The Bishop's Jaegers* had been adapted for the stage by Bertrand Robinson, but, apparently, unlike the stage adaptation of *Turnabout*, the play was never produced.[36]

The storylines of the novels may be of Thorne Smith's times, but the ideas and the concepts belong to all time. The political incorrectness of the Thorne Smith stories — the emphasis on alcoholic consumption on female underwear and on general and unrestrained licentious behavior — is a breath of pure fresh air in today's straitlaced world.

THE INFLUENCE OF THORNE SMITH'S WRITINGS ON LATER NOVELS

The Thorne Smith influence extends beyond film, television and the theatre to the novel itself. Arguments can easily be made that many writers have been directly or indirectly influenced by the author of *Topper*. There are the comic, science fiction books by James P. Blaylock, although there is much that disturbs rather than entertains here. A member of the "Beat" generation and largely forgotten today, Richard Brautigan has been compared to Thorne Smith. The novels of Rudy Rucker have been described as "zany" and "weird," although his influences, it is claimed, are Kurt Vonnegut and William S. Burroughs, rather than Thorne Smith. John D. MacDonald's *The Girl, the Gold Watch & Everything* (1962), with its story of a man who inherits a gold pocket watch that stops time for everyone but its owner, has a close affinity to Thorne Smith's writings.

Another novelist sometimes mentioned as writing in the Thorne Smith tradition is Richard Matheson. In particular two of his books, *Bid Time Return* (1975), filmed as *Somewhere in Time* and later reprinted under that title, and *What Dreams May Come True* (1978) are singled out. In fact Matheson's approach to the supernatural is more scientific and devoid of humor. There is too much darkness and not enough light in his writings for Matheson to claim a Thorne Smith connection.

While there is nothing supernatural about his work, a writer far more outrageously in the Thorne Smith tradition is Patrick Dennis (1921-1976). Dennis wrote many novels, some under the pseudonym of Virginia Rowans, and he is best remembered for *Auntie Mame* (1955), which has much the same humor and style as a Thorne Smith book. He is as "camp" as Smith and more gay (in the modern sense of the word). Like Smith, he was a heavy drinker. Like Smith, Dennis was part of the Greenwich Village literary scene. And, like Smith, he is somewhat out of fashion.

One writer with a close affinity to Thorne Smith, whose career took off shortly after the latter's death is James Thurber (1894-1961). As did Smith, Thurber used his writings to point out human frailties, with weak men and strong women. And like Smith, Thurber displayed a fondness for dogs. Thurber's most famous work is the 1939 story "The Secret Life of Walter Mitty," first published in *The New Yorker*, whose central character is a daydreamer very much in the fashion of Topper. The story, of course, formed the basis for a 1940 Broadway production, *The Male Animal*, and for a 1947 Danny Kaye film.

One modern novel, while not a great literary achievement, stands out as being in the Thorne Smith style, and that is *Imagine Me and You* by Billy Mernit (2008). The central character here is a Hollywood screenwriter who creates a character in his script with whom he falls in love and whom only he can see. The screenwriter lives his life as the star of a romantic comedy in which he is played by Cary Grant and his imagined girlfriend by Katharine Hepburn.

As Paul Di Filippo has written,

"If one were to attempt to fabricate a writer from bits and pieces of Charles Bukowski, S.J. Perelman, Damon Runyon, Lewis Carroll and Mark Twain, one might possibly come close to creating a figure like Thorne Smith. But such a chimera would still surely not possess the original's high-spirited elan, sense of utter irresponsibility and fine disdain for all forms of convention — traits which found their perfect embodiment in a series of 'ribald' screwball novels where the fantastic plays a pivotal part in disrupting society, unleashing repressed individuals with shattering unnatural strictures."[37]

There are too many artists of all manner and media influenced by Smith or who indirectly shaped his stories. The Marx Brothers from the worlds of vaudeville, theatre and film immediately come to mind, for example, but who really influenced who? Monty Python, with the appearance of the Spanish Inquisition into present-day society, might owe something to Thorne Smith.

The reality is that while Thorne Smith and his comedic writings might originate in the age of prohibition and depression, they resonate today as much as always for those who take the time, and have the enthusiasm, to seek them out. The reader will immediately determine a link between the humor of the novels and the comedic antics of our current entertainers and writers. The last will find much to emulate and repackage in Thorne Smith's work. Perhaps some elements of the stories have dated but the comic underpinnings reverberate today and will be as modern as tomorrow.

1. H. Allen Smith, People Named Smith, p. 182.

2. Roland Young and Thorne Smith among Others, Thorne Smith: His Life and Times, p. 29.

3. Ibid, p. 19.

4. Topper, p. 212.

5. The New York Times accidentally titles the book The Glorious Fool, which might well have served as a description of Thorne Smith himself.

6. The Glorious Pool, p. 3

7. Ibid, p. 36.

8. Joan Kahn, New York Times, March 28, 1943, p. BR14.

9. The Glorious Pool, p. 297, and the last words in the novel.

10. Undated Kirkus review on file in the Literature Department of the Los Angeles Central Library.

11. Information taken from Michael D. Walker, "Host to Said Ghosts: The Thorne Smith Story," p. 47.

12. Quoted in Joseph Leo Blotner, Thorne Smith: A Study in Popular Fiction, p. 102.

13. Linda Ben-Zvi, Susan Glaspell: Her Life and Times, New York: Oxford University Press, 2005, p. 357.

14. The Passionate Witch, p. 24.

15. Ibid, p. 110.

16. Roland Young unpublished, untitled and unpaged autobiography.

17. With too many films awaiting release, the studio decided to dispose of some to United Artists. Other films in the package, also designated Cinema Guild productions, were The Crystal Ball and Young and Willing, as well as as group of Harry Sherman-produced Westerns, including six Hopalong Cassidy features and the Richard Dix Western American Empire.

18. Bats in the Belfry, p. 45.

19. I would be remiss if I did not also note that "Bats in the Belfy" is used to describe a certain sexual position. In that the novel was not written by Thorne Smith, it is quite irrelevant as to whether or not he was familiar with the term or, for that matter, the position.

20. Bats in the Belfy, pp. 43-44.

21. Ibid, p. 44.

22. Brian Stableford, "Matson, Norman H(aghejm)," p. 393.

23. Rain in the Doorway in The Thorne Smith 3-Decker, p. 494.

24. Ibid, p. 495.

25. John Mulryan, "Thorne Smith: 1892-1934," p. 1439.

26. The Sun Dial Press was an imprint of Doubleday, Doran, publishing "quality" hardcover books.

27. Undated Kirkus review on file in the Literature Department of the Los Angeles Central Library.

28. Carl Van Doren, The American Novel: 1789-1939, pp. 331-332.

29. Joseph Blotner to Anthony Slide, September 1, 2009.

30. "The Boss's Breeches," July 1954, pp. 6-9, 12-18, 36, 41-42, 45-46; "The Adventures of Hector," October 1955, pp. 6-10, 16, 20, 27, 34, 36, 43-44, 48, 50, 59, 62. "The Boss's Breeches" was also included in The Best from Playboy, edited by Hugh Hefner (Waldorf Publishing Company, 1954).

31. Howard Steven Jitomir, Forgotten Excellence: A Study of Thorne Smith's Humor, pp. 221-223.

32. Topper, p. 144.

33. Katherine A. Fowkes, Giving Up the Ghost: Spirits, Ghosts, and Angels in Mainstream Comedy Films, p. 178.

34. The play subsequently opened in New York in 1941 and was filmed in 1945; Margaret Rutherford became a star as a result of her performance as Madame Arcati in both the original London production and the screen adaptation.

35. "Coward Pulls a Topper," New York Times, July 13, 1941, p. X1.

36. New York Times, October 2, 1935, p. 27.

37. Paul Di Filippo, "Smith, Thorne," p. 533.

BIBLIOGRAPHY

Sources cited in full in the endnotes are not included here.

Benet, W.R. and N.H. Pearson. *The Oxford Anthology of American Literature*. New York: Oxford University Press, 1945.

Blotner, Joseph Leo. *Thorne Smith: A Study in Popular Fiction*. PhD dissertation, University of Pennsylvania, 1951.

Cowley, Malcolm, ed. *Writers at Work: The Paris Review Interviews*. New York: The Viking Press, 1958.

Di Filippo, Paul, "Smith, Thorne," in ed. David Pringle, *St. James Guide to Fantasy Writers*. New York: St. James Press, 1996.

Dunning, John. *Tune in Yesterday: The Ultimate Encyclopedia of Old-Time Radio, 1925-1976*. Englewood Cliffs, N.J.: Prentice-Hall, 1976.

Fowkes, Katherine A. *Giving Up the Ghost: Spirits, Ghosts, and Angels in Mainstream Comedy Films*. Detroit: Wayne State University Press, 1998.

Freeman, Lewis, "Paper-Bound Books in America – Part II," *Publishers Weekly*, November 23, 1952, pp. 2081-2085.

Goldin, Stephen, "The Stray Lamb," in ed. Frank N. Magill, *Survey of Modern Fantasy Literature*, vol. 4, pp. 1848-1850. Englewood Cliffs, N.J.: Salem Press, 1983.

_____, "Topper and Topper Takes a Trip," ibid, vol. 5, pp. 1958-1962. Englewood Cliffs, N.J.: Salem Press, 1983.

_____, "Turnabout," ibid, vol. 5, pp. 1983-1985. Englewood Cliffs, N.J.: Salem Press, 1983.

Hackett, Alice Payne and James Henry Burke. *80 Years of Best Sellers: 1895-1957*. New York: R.R. Bowker, 1977.

Hanke, Ken, "*Topper Returns*," *Scarlet Street*, No. 37, 2000, pp. 54-59, 75-76.

Hanson, Patricia King, ed. *The American Film Institute Catalog of Motion Pictures Produced in the United States: Feature Films, 1931-1940*. Berkeley: University of California Press, 1993.

_____. *The American Film Institute Catalog of Motion Pictures Produced in the United States: Feature Films, 1941-1950*. Berkeley: University of California Press, 1999.

Harryhausen, Ray and Tony Dalton. *Ray Harryhausen: An Animated Life*. New York: Billboard Books, 2003.

Hart, James D. *The Popular Book: A History of America's Literary Taste*. New York: Oxford University Press, 1950.

Hoppenstand, Gary, "Murder and Other Acts of High Society," *The Armchair Detective*, fall 1993, pp. 63-68.

Jitomir, Howard Steven. *Forgotten Excellence: A Study of Thorne Smith's Humor*. PhD dissertation, St. John's University (New York), 1983.

Langford, David, "Smith (James) Thorne (Jr)," in ed. John Clute and John Grant, *The Encyclopedia of Fantasy*, p. 881. New York: St. Martin's Press, 1997.

Mott, Frank Luther. *Golden Multitudes: The Story of Best-Sellers in the United States*. New York: Macmillan, 1947.

Mulryan, John, "Thorne Smith: 1892-1934," in ed. Walton Beacham and Suzanne Niemeyer, *Popular World Fiction, 1900 – Present*, vol. 4, Washington, D.C. Beacham Publishing, 1987, pp. 1439-1445.

Scott, John, "Amazing New Camera Tricks Developed by Screen Magicians," *Los Angeles Times*, April 25, 1937, p. C1.

See, Carolyn, "Introduction," to *Topper*, New York: Modern Library, 1999, pp. ix-xiv.

Seymour, Blackie, "Pentagram Profiles: *Night Life of the Gods*," *Classic Images*, March 1997, pp. 30-31.

Smith, H. Allen. *People Named Smith*. Garden City, N.Y.: Doubleday, 1950.

Stableford, Brian, "Matson, Norman H (aghejm)," in ed. David Pringle, *St. James Guide to Fantasy Writers*, pp. 392-393. New York: St. James Press, 1996.

Stearns, Harold. *The Confessions of a Harvard Man: The Street I Know*. Santa Barbara, Ca.: The Paget Press, 1984.

Thornesmith.net.

"Thorne Smith: Haunts and By-Paths" website.

Thurber, James. *The Years with Ross*. Boston: Little, Brown, 1959.

Van Doren, Carl. *The American Novel: 1789-1939*. New York: Macmillan, 1947.

Veale, Scott, "Drinking Gin with the Dead," *New York Times Book Review*, September 20, 2000, p. 47.

Walker, Michael D., "Host to Said Ghosts: The Thorne Smith Story," *Scarlet Street*, No. 37, 2000, pp. 40-49, 74.

Watson, Christine, "The Night Life of the Gods," in ed. Frank N. Magill, *Survey of Modern Fantasy Literature*, volume 3, pp. 1111-1115. Englewood Cliffs, N.J.: Salem Press, 1983.

Whitlock, Stephen, "A Fanciful Haunting Tale of Influence," *New York Times*, October 19, 1997, pp. 13, 18.

Yamane, Linus, "Free Acres," pzcad.pitzer.edu.

Young, Roland, and Thorne Smith among Others. *Thorne Smith: His Life and Times with a Note on His Books & A Complete Bibliography*. Garden City, N.Y.: Doubleday, Doran, 1934.

THE COMPLETE WORKS
OF THORNE SMITH

Biltmore Oswald: The Diary of a Hapless Recruit (by J. Thorne Smith, Jr., U.S.N.R.F.). New York: Frederick A. Stokes, published on November 4, 1918. 87 pages. Registered for copyright, A506541, on November 11, 1918. Copyright has expired. Reprinted from *The Broadside*.

Out o' Luck: Biltmore Oswald Very Much at Sea (by J. Thorne Smith, Jr., U.S.N.R.F.). New York: Frederick A. Stokes, published on June 16, 1919. 120 pages. Registered for copyright, A515936, on June 20, 1919. Copyright has expired. Reprinted from *The Broadside*.

Haunts and By-Paths and Other Poems (by J. Thorne Smith, Jr.). New York: Frederick A. Stokes, published on September 19, 1919. 139 pages. Registered for copyright, A530944, on September 24, 1919. Copyright has expired.

"Advertising," in *Civilization in the United States: An Inquiry by Thirty Americans*, editor Harold E. Stearns (by J. Thorne Smith). New York: Harcourt, Brace, published on January 5, 1922, pp. 381-395. Registered for copyright, A654475, on February 3, 1922. Copyright has expired.

Topper: An Improbable Adventure. New York: Robert M. McBride, published on February 20, 1926. 292 pages. Registered for copyright, A879717, on February 26, 1926. Copyright renewed, R107928, on February 24, 1953. Published in London in 1926 by Robert Holden. Reprinted in 1933 by Doubleday, Doran. Reprinted in London in 1933 as *The Jovial Ghosts: The Misadventures of Topper* by Arthur Barker. Cheap hardcover edition published in Garden City, New York, in 1933 by Sun Dial Press. Reprinted in 1936 by Grosset and Dunlap. Paperback edition published in New York in 1939 by Pocket Books. Paperback edition published in New York in 1999 by Modern Library.

Dream's End. New York: Robert M. McBride, published on March 25, 1927. 342 pages. Registered for copyright, A972832, on April 21, 1927. Copyright renewed, R143390, on January 24, 1944. Published in London in 1928 by Jarrolds. Reprinted in 1933 by Robert M. McBride.

The Stray Lamb. New York: Cosmopolitan Book Corporation, published on September 21, 1929. 303 pages. Registered for copyright, A13533, on September 23, 1929. Copyright renewed, R177692, on September 25, 1956. Published in London in 1930 by William Heinemann. Reprinted in 1932 by Doubleday, Doran. Cheap hardcover edition published in Garden City, New York, in 1942 by Sun Dial Press. Paperback edition published in New York in 1948 by Pocket Books.

Did She Fall? New York: Cosmopolitan Book Corporation, published on August 14, 1930. 286 pages. Registered for copyright, A26702, on August 15, 1930. Copyright renewed, R197338, on August 15, 1957. Reprinted in August 1932 by Doubleday, Doran. Published in London in 1936 by Arthur Barker. Cheap hardcover edition published in Garden City, New York, in 1937 by Sun Dial Press. Paperback edition published in New York in 1947 by Pocket Books.

The Night Life of the Gods. Garden City, N.Y.: Doubleday, Doran, published on March 20, 1931. 311 pages. Registered for copyright, A36245, on April 2, 1931. Copyright renewed, R211681, on March 26, 1958. Published in London in 1934 by Arthur Barker. Cheap hardcover edition published in Garden City, New York, in 1939 by Sun Dial Press. Paperback edition published in New York in 1947 by Pocket Books. Paperback edition published in 1999 by Modern Library.

Turnabout. Garden City, N.Y.: Doubleday, Doran, published on September 24, 1931. 312 pages. Registered for copyright, A42975, on September 28, 1931. Copyright renewed, R222071, on September 29, 1958. Published in London in 1933 by Arthur Barker. Cheap hardcover edition published in Garden City, New York, in 1940, by Sun Dial Press. Paperback edition published in New York in 1947 by Pocket Books.

Lazy Bear Lane. Garden City, N.Y.: Doubleday, Doran, published on November 5, 1931. 240 pages. Registered for copyright, A44980, on November 16, 1931. Copyright renewed, R225060, on November 19, 1958.

Topper Takes a Trip. Garden City, N.Y.: Doubleday, Doran, published on May 5, 1932. 325 pages. Registered for copyright, A51323, on May 16, 1932. Copyright renewed, R236361, on May 6, 1959. Published in London in 1935 by Arthur Barker. Cheap hardcover edition published in Garden City, New York, in 1937 by Sun Dial Press. Paperback edition published in 1999 by Modern Library. A new version of this book was registered for copyright A575832, citing a publication date of May 15, 1962, by Pyramid Books. The registration, which protected only new matter described as "new pictorial and editorial revisions" was renewed, RE585-475 on December 19, 1990.

The Bishop's Jaegers. Garden City, N.Y.: Doubleday, Doran, published on October 26, 1932. 311 pages. Registered for copyright, A55813, on November 5, 1932. Copyright renewed, R244634, on October 27, 1959. Published in London in 1934 by Arthur Barker. Cheap hardcover edition published in Garden City, New York, in 1939 by Sun Dial Press. Paperback edition published in New York in 1945 by Pocket Books.

Rain in the Doorway. Garden City, N.Y.: Doubleday, Doran, published on April 12, 1933. 304 pages. Published with a special Thorne Smith bookplate: "KLEPTOMANIAC'S EDITION. What happens when you sit down in the evening to enjoy a new Thorne Smith? Like Topper's ghost, it's disappeared! Some friend has – *borrowed* – your copy. Now as a first-aid to the harassed book owner, we have devised a bookplate. Detach, sign, and paste in your copy of Thorne Smith...and if the book is ever caught on anyone else, *will his face be red*!" Registered for copyright, A62226, on April 15, 1933. Copyright renewed, R255957, on April 26, 1960. Published in London in 1933 by Arthur Barker. Cheap hardcover edition published in Garden City, New York, in 1937 by Sun Dial Press. Paperback edition published in New York in 1949 by Pocket Books.

Skin and Bones. Garden City, N.Y.: Doubleday, Doran, published on December 17, 1933. 300 pages. Registered for copyright, A68876, on January 2, 1934. Copyright renewed, R268405, on December 28, 1960. Published in London in 1936 by Arthur Barker. Cheap hardcover edition published in Garden City, New York, in 1939 by Sun Dial Press. Paperback edition published in New York in 1948 by Pocket Books.

"Yonder's Henry!," *Esquire*, Volume One, Number Three, February 1934, pp. 34-35, 102, 105, 112.

Thorne Smith: His Life and Times with a Note on His Books & a Complete Bibliography by Roland Young and Thorne Smith among Others. Garden City, N.Y.: Doubleday, Doran, 1934. Paperback Monograph. No copyright registration or renewal. The initial essay here is credited to M.J., who is editor Malcolm Johnson, and to whom credit should probably go as primary author.

The Glorious Pool. Garden City, N.Y.: Doubleday, Doran, published on December 19, 1934. 292 pages. Registered for copyright, A78798, on December 21, 1934. Copyright renewed, R28237, on December 20, 1961. Published in London in 1935 by Arthur Barker. Cheap hardcover edition published in Garden City, New York, in 1938 by Sun Dial Press. Paperback edition published in New York in 1946 by Pocket Books.

The Thorne Smith 3-Decker. Garden City, N.Y.: Doubleday, Doran, 1936. Includes *The Stray Lamb*, *Turnabout* and *Rain in the Doorway*. Also published by the Literary Guild, and in cheap hardcover edition by Sun Dial Press.

The Thorne Smith Triplets. Garden City, N.Y.: Doubleday, Doran, 1938. Includes *Topper Takes a Trip*, *The Night Life of the Gods* and *The Bishop's Jaegers*. Also published by the Literary Guild, and in cheap hardcover edition by Sun Dial Press.

The Passionate Witch (completed by Norman Matson). Garden City, N.Y.: Doubleday, Doran, published on July 25, 1941. 267 pages. Registered for copyright, A157941, on October 7, 1941. Copyright renewed, R44133, on August 22, 1968. Published in London in 1942 by Methuen.

Cheap hardcover edition published in Garden City, New York, in 1942 by Sun Dial Press. Paperback edition published in New York in 1946 by Pocket Books.

Bats in the Belfry (written by Norman Matson as a sequel to *The Passionate Witch*). Garden City, N.Y.: Doubleday, Doran, published on May 7, 1943. 242 pages. Registered for copyright, A173125, on May 13, 1943. Copyright renewed, R484290, on May 11, 1970.

The Thorne Smith Three-Bagger. Garden City, N.Y.: Doubleday, Doran, 1943. Includes *The Glorious Pool, Skin and Bones* and *Topper.* Also published by the Literary Guild, and in cheap hardcover edition by Sun Dial Press.

THE FILMS
OF THORNE SMITH

Menu. A Metro-Goldwyn-Mayer production, released August 1933.
Story by Thorne Smith. Director: Nick Grinde. Narrator: Pete Smith.
10 minutes.
   With Una Merkel, Franklin Pangborn and Luis Alberni.

Night Life of the Gods. A Universal Pictures production, released
March 1935. Based on the novel *The Night Life of the Gods*. Producer:
Carl Laemmle, Jr. Director: Lowell Sherman. Screenplay: Barry Triv-
ers. Cinematography: John J. Mescall. Special Effects: John P. Fulton. 73
minutes.
   With Alan Mowbray, Florine McKinney, Peggy Shannon, Richard
Carle, Theresa Maxwell Conover, Phillips Smalley, Wesley Barry, Gilbert
Emery, Henry Armetta, and Robert Warwick.

Topper. A Hal Roach production, released by Metro-Goldwyn-Mayer,
July 1937. Based on the novel of the same name. Producer: Hal Roach.
Director: Norman Z. McLeod. Screenplay: Jack Jevne, Eric Hatch and
Eddie Moran. Cinematography: Norbert Brodine. Special Photographic
Effects: Roy Seawright. 98 minutes.
   With Constance Bennett, Cary Grant, Roland Young, Billie Burke,
Alan Mowbray, Eugene Pallette, Arthur Lake, Hedda Hopper, Virginia
Sale, Theodore von Eltz, and J. Farrell MacDonald.

Topper Takes a Trip. A Hal Roach production, released by United Artists, January 1939. Based on the novel of the same name. Producer: Milton
H. Bren. Director: Norman Z. McLeod. Screenplay: Eddie Moran, Jack

Jevne and Corey Ford. Cinematography: Norbert Brodine. Special Photographic Effects: Roy Seawright. 85 minutes.

With Constance Bennett, Roland Young, Billie Burke, Alan Mowbray, Verree Teasdale, Franklin Pangborn, Alexander D'Arcy, and Paul Hurst.

Turnabout. A Hal Roach production, released by United Artists, May 1940. Based on the novel of the same name. Producer: Hal Roach. Director: Hal Roach. Screenplay: Mickell Novak, Berne Giler and John McClain. Additional Dialogue: Rian James. Cinematography: Norbert Brodine. Special Photographic Effects: Roy Seawright. 83 minutes.

With Adolphe Menjou, Carole Landis, John Hubbard, William Gargan, Verree Teasdale, Mary Astor, Donald Meek, Joyce Compton, Inez Courtney, Franklin Pangborn, Marjorie Main, and Berton Churchill.

Topper Returns. A Hal Roach production, released by United Artists, March 1941. Based on characters created by Thorne Smith. Producer: Hal Roach. Director: Roy Del Ruth. Screenplay: Jonathan Latimer and Gordon Douglas. Additional Dialogue: Paul Gerard Smith. Cinematography: Norbert Brodine. Special Photographic Effects: Roy Seawright. 95 minutes.

With Joan Blondell, Roland Young, Carole Landis, Billie Burke, Dennis O'Keefe, Patsy Kelly, H.B. Warner, and Eddie "Rochester" Anderson.

I Married a Witch. A Cinema Guild and René Clair production for Paramount, released by United Artists, October 1942. Based on the novel, *The Passionate Witch.* Producer: Preston Sturges. Director: René Clair. Screenplay: Robert Pirosh and Marc Connelly. Cinematography: Ted Tetzlaff. Special Photographic Effects: Gordon Jennings. 82 minutes.

With Fredric March, Veronica Lake, Robert Benchley, Susan Hayward, Cecil Kellaway, Elizabeth Patterson, and Robert Warwick.

INDEX

THORNE SMITH

HIS LIFE AND TIMES

koese

THORNE SMITH:

HIS LIFE AND TIMES

WITH A NOTE ON HIS

BOOKS & A COMPLETE

BIBLIOGRAPHY · BY

ROLAND YOUNG AND

THORNE SMITH AMONG

OTHERS

DOUBLEDAY, DORAN

A NOTE ON
MR. SMITH'S
LIFE AND
TIMES

T WAS SOME TIME in 1929 that Thorne Smith's present publishers began to grow acutely conscious of a new legend gathering force in American letters. It concerned two rather mysterious books which well-informed people were telling each other about with eager enthusiasm. One dealt with a man who got himself involved with a lot of ghosts; not the kind that rattled chains on the bastions of old castles and went who-o-o-o in the midnight, but the gayest and most ribald of creatures, who saw no reason for being divorced from earthly pleasures simply because they were on another astral plane; its title was TOPPER. The other was equally fantastic, but in it were no ghosts. Instead a harried commuter, named Lamb, easily recognisable as almost any one of us, struggled through its pages in a wild riot of adventures stemming from the fact that an odd little man Mr. Lamb had met in the woods kept turning him into a variety of animals. That was THE STRAY LAMB.

The most casual reading of these two books, whose first editions were even then being collected by knowing bibliophiles, was sufficient to explain the growth of the legend. They were like no other novels ever written. They sprang, like MOBY DICK, out of the soil and the life of America, but their roots were in the earth and not in other books. They were native fairy-tales, but at the same time they were satire of a high order. More than either, they were fun to read and reread. Repetition staled none of their gayety, their perception of the tragedies and absurdities of existence. As all of his books have been since, they were suffused with a kindly magic which enabled the characters and the reader alike to escape for a little from the crushing problems of existence, from the lives of quiet desperation, which, as Thoreau once pointed out in an immortal line, the majority of men and women are destined to lead. His men and women wandered in a new and better world, in a modern, adult fairyland, for his characters were Scheherazade's califs and beggars, they were Gulliver in Lilliput, they were Hansel and Gretel in the enchanted wood.

Further investigation disclosed the fact that the man who had brought this new world into being had, earlier, written two of the war years' most famous books, BILTMORE OSWALD and OUT O' LUCK, forming together the wistful and yet side-splitting saga of a naval recruit; a book of verse, HAUNTS AND BY-PATHS; and a serious, lovely, introspective novel, DREAM'S END. Still further research disclosed the author himself, hidden away in New Jersey with his wife and two children. His house, characteristically, was built around trees which occupied most of the rooms.

Shortly thereafter Thorne Smith returned to New York and began to write his new novel. The result was THE NIGHT LIFE OF THE GODS, now in its 12th edition, and, three years after publication, what publishers call a steady stock item, by which they mean that month in and month out hundreds

4

of new readers discover and buy it, that it is one of those rare books that stores must carry on their shelves at all times.

With it the legend took on new impetus. Its mad and astonishing account of the man who discovered how to change statues into people, and Meg, the 900 year old trollop who knew the other side of the secret—how to turn *people* into *statues*, promptly outstripped the previous books in popularity. The critics remained a little puzzled at the whole thing, and only the most astute among them gave it more than a condescending glance. Meanwhile editions melted quietly away, and by the time TURNABOUT was completed it was apparent that a new master of humor and fantasy had come to stay, that the Thorne Smith legend would become a part of our literary history.

TURNABOUT took the commonest remark in the American household, whether addressed by husband to wife or vice versa: "If I could only be in *your* shoes for one day!" and calmly turned it into an accomplished fact. Tim and Sally, its chief protagonists, found themselves one day not only in each other's shoes, but in each other's bodies. During the wild fantasia of mixed sexes which ensued, a sharp and searching wit examined the whole panorama of suburban life, cocktail parties, big business, marriage, and a good many other of the more important phases of modern manners. Twenty-first century delvers into literary history are going to be delighted with TURNABOUT. Its picture of life in the third decade of this century is so appallingly exact that it will hopelessly confuse the historians of the future. As a matter of record, it promptly doubled the sales of its immediate predecessor and is being discovered, with loud whoops of joy, by nearly ten thousand new readers annually.

After TURNABOUT have come, lit with unfailing wit, incubated by an endlessly fertile imagination, a series of

5

equally extraordinary books—TOPPER TAKES A TRIP, THE BISHOP'S JAEGERS (the tempestuous tale of a nudist colony which set such a fashion that imitations have been appearing regularly ever since), RAIN IN THE DOORWAY, SKIN AND BONES. In process of completion is THE GLORIOUS POOL, and in Thorne Smith's note-books are plans for a dozen more new books.

At this point the author, who will have a chance to speak for himself later on, deserves some slight consideration. Like his work, Thorne Smith is an inescapable joy. He is the kindliest, the least sophisticated (in the accepted sense) man in New York. His fondness for dogs (his books are full of the most beguiling and clumsy dogs, Oscar, Busy, Dopey, a veritable kennel of them) cats, guppies, zoos and even children is proverbial, as is his penchant for hard work, foreign travel and detective stories. Strangely enough his reading, except for the criminal element, is mostly serious, selected from such authors as Wassermann, Knut Hamsun, Nëxo, Rolland, William Beebe, and a number of writers on travel and exploration. If he can help it he never reads a so-called funny book, including his own.

He is delighted by the fact that his younger daughter has so far baffled every educational system with which she has become involved. His elder daughter has started her first novel—several times. Mr. Smith says he wishes he had written some of its passages himself.

Although he carries a stick on the street, he wears as little as possible at home, frequently one of the curious shirts to be bought in France, of the kind Tim Williams wore in TURNABOUT.

Of all authors we know he is perhaps the least aware of himself or of what he has done. And it is only on rare and

A malicious and untruthful sketch by the actor, Roland Young, of the author, Thorne Smith, who as a matter of fact, in real life is often confused with John Barrymore.

unexpected occasions that he startles his publishers and every-one else within ear-shot by his sudden and furious declara-tions of his place in the sun. A few kind words or the slight gift of a book usually restores him to his customary state of good nature. He seldom frequents night-clubs and is not happy at large gatherings. He dislikes stuffed shirts and pro-fessional wise-crackers. He prefers his small estate in New Jersey to his city apartment, and the soft coasts of southern France to either.

7

How he came to be an author at all is not very clear. The sea is in his blood, and by rights he should by now be an admiral. His father was Commodore James Thorne Smith, U. S. N., supervisor of the port of New York during the war, his great grandfather, Don Jose Maxwell of Rio de Janeiro, fleet owner and coffee planter, and he himself was born at the Naval Academy at Annapolis, Maryland.

That was on an unspecified month in 1892. From then on his career has been marked by a certain unconventionality, beginning with the incident of being completely mislaid a few months after his birth. The place was the vast railroad station at Baltimore, the mislayer a nurse-maid in a state of faintly alcoholic abstraction, and as a result he has since seldom been able to catch a train or keep an appointment within a radius of at least two days.

He was educated at Locust Dale Academy in Virginia, at St. Luke's School, Wayne, Pennsylvania, and at Dartmouth College, and after that went into advertising. The war intervened then, and enlisting as a common sailor he rose straightly to chief bos'uns mate. He has never explained that rise, but it involved also the assumption of the editorship of the *Broadside*, a Naval Reserve publication. There appeared, in the course of time, a series of pieces which the astute house of Stokes saw, gathered into book form, and, under the title of BILTMORE OSWALD, sold some seventy thousand copies. It was Thorne Smith's first book, and its first editions are now held at prohibitive prices. OUT O' LUCK, a sequel, followed it to success, but by that time the author, racked by a long illness, had seen the war end, and was going on to other fields.

For two years he dwelt at the Greenwich Village Inn in company with Sinclair Lewis, John Reed, Barney Gallant, Harold Stearns, Jack Conroy, and various other stout spirits.

8

Poems, for one thing, were the chief product of that period. They appeared in the old *Smart Set*, the *Liberator*, and various newspapers, and late in 1919 were brought together in HAUNTS AND BY-PATHS. There was a bride to support by that time and with royalties exhausted and the verse market unsatisfactory, he went back to advertising. The lucky agency was E. B. Wilson, Inc., financial specialists, and so proud were they of the association, or so relieved at its termination, that he was presented on leaving with a gold wrist-watch. During that and the tenure of other similiar positions, his manuscripts were being rejected with regularity by the better-known publishers.

Finally, while copy executive at Doremus & Company (he had been frightened away from J. Walter Thompson by the combination of a questionnaire and moorish gates) he finished DREAM'S END, and once more approached the publishers. They were cold, but undiscouraged, he set about a new kind of story, the tale mentioned earlier, about a man who fell in love with a ghost. The immortal TOPPER was born, DREAM'S END followed it shortly, and a literary career had begun in real earnest.

Thorne Smith has given the world laughter, a gift not lightly to be dismissed. That is the reason why TOPPER and all the novels since are still in print, why more people every year buy each one of them rather than buy the whole output of the average novel. Of the significance of the things that lie beneath the surface of that laughter there is no need to ponder very deeply here. His impact on the American scene has been enormous. He has attacked with vehemence every form of hypocrisy, he has examined with sympathy and insight our universal neuroses. He has written about sex without shame and without a leer, and his work has done as

9

much to destroy sham and pretense on that subject as has Havelock Ellis's. And he has accomplished all this with hilarious good humor, with a wise and sun-lit gaiety.

Harry Emerson Wildes once said in the Philadelphia *Public-Ledger*, "When I come to be dictator I'm going to have all books burned but Thorne Smith's and Wodehouse's. Then we'll rebuild civilization anew with them as a basis and we'll have Utopia." And a Utopia it would be indeed, the Utopia a tired world needs and would understand—but one which would probably bring the world to a swift but hilarious end, which perhaps is as it should be.

M. J.

This picture is complicated by the revolver, the starfish and the empty champagne bottles. Or maybe it is simplified by them. At any rate, TOPPER TAKES A TRIP explains all, if you can call it an explanation. The person with the gun is a ghost, by the way. Would you have known it?

This lady, who seems to be annoyed by something other than her lack of raiment, is to be met with in the pages of TOPPER TAKES A TRIP. She isn't very moral, but nobody seems very perturbed by that, and you'll undoubtedly have a different outlook on life after meeting her.

ROLAND YOUNG IS FORCED TO INTERVIEW THORNE SMITH

It should be understood that this interview with Thorne Smith by Roland Young was not of Mr. Young's seeking. It was forced on him by the author himself. Having lunched with their usual moderation at Tony's, Roland Young found Thorne Smith looking wistfully at him over the rim of his glass. Mr. Young, priding himself on being surprised at nothing, and especially at nothing connected with Thorne Smith, wanted to know what was wrong now.

MR. SMITH: Come, come, Mr Young. You must not let this get the best of you. Ask me a question.

MR. YOUNG: (*brightening visibly*): How about a Scotch and soda?

MR. SMITH: That's not a question. It's a foregone conclusion. Try again. Interview me!

MR. YOUNG: Why should I interview you?

MR. SMITH: Well, I feel as if somebody should interview me. Nobody ever has, successfully, and I feel terribly uninterviewed. It's almost as embarrassing as being caught naked in public.

MR. YOUNG: Like your characters?

MR. SMITH: Let's forget my characters.

MR. YOUNG: I wish I could. I'll try to confine my interview to you.

MR. SMITH: Shall we call ourselves Mr. Smith and Mr. Young in this interview?

MR. YOUNG: If we stick to that I think we'll be safe. Mr. Smith, have you a birth certificate?

MR. SMITH: No.

MR. YOUNG: That's what I thought. You haven't a birth certificate, so how do you know you were born at all? Isn't it barely possible that you wrote yourself into being? Sometimes I'm inclined to believe that you're only another character out of your books.

MR. SMITH: I often wish I were. They always seem to have a rather merry time of it.

MR. YOUNG: Are your books planned or do they just grow?

12

MR. SMITH: My books are planned in stealth, and grow in desperation.

MR. YOUNG: Then like folklore they just grow, as do some of our comic strips in the newspapers. What I'm trying to get at is that I've often run across you in the comic strips—especially in Mr. Herriman's *Krazy Kat*.

MR. SMITH: I'm afraid you are getting somewhere.

MR. YOUNG: I know I am. That's what I want to talk about. For years I've been bored with the arty attitude so many people take to American folklore. I've been bored with all this self-conscious stuff about Paul Bunyan, Scotch ballads slightly done over for cowboy use, precious books about Kentucky mountaineers. That isn't the true American folklore. The true folklore isn't planned as such. It just grows, like some of our comic strips or like the *Three Little Pigs* in the movies or Amos and Andy on the radio. It expresses in the most ridiculous way the deep-seated instincts of the people, their hidden desperations, their craving for laughter and a free sort of beauty.

Just to show that Roland Young, in addition to being a great actor and inter-viewer is also a distinguished artist and author, the illustration below is offered with its explanatory verse. It appears in *Not for Children*, which is a pleasant book to have around the house on rainy days.

THE FLEA

And here's the happy, bounding flea—
You cannot tell the he from she.
The sexes look alike, you see;
But she can tell and so can he.

	Also, their badly controlled impatience with convention and smug hypocrisy.
MR. SMITH:	Go on, Mr. Young. I don't understand you at all, but it sounds highly flattering.
MR. YOUNG:	There's always something a little sad in even the maddest of your books—something a little bitter and at the same time rather gallantly goofy in the face of inevitable defeat. *Turnabout*, for instance, is a complete answer to the commonest remark in the American home, "I wish you had to lead my life for just one day!" Just as *Topper* or *Rain in the Doorway* expressed the secret ambitions that practically all men have if they're healthy. Your books baffle some reviewers because they lack either the time or perception to take your humor seriously. In a sense it is the humor of desperation and disillusionment. Instead of sobbing about it, you laugh. With a few exceptions they don't seem to know what to make of you. They don't seem to understand that you are one of the most original manifestations in American literature for many years Some day they will.
MR. SMITH:	You mean after I'm——?
MR. YOUNG:	(*sadly*): Yes. I'm afraid so.
MR. SMITH:	(*brokenly*): Another Scotch and soda.
MR. YOUNG:	You're the least derivative author I've ever read. I can't find out your literary ancestors— that's why I think you must be mad. Although your books are essentially fairy tales for adults they are thoroughly a part of life, in some instances grimly realistic.

14

MR. SMITH: Well, I'll tell you. When I was a nipper I led a sort of solitary, dreamlike existence. A dearth of playmates. To compensate for this I used to endow my playthings—mostly stuffed Brownies—with life. Finally I became so batty I actually thought they were alive. When my older brother discovered this secret existence of mine he very thriftily turned it to his advantage. This young devil succeeded in

The duck is named Havelock Ellis, and he seems to be biting the young woman, not very politely, possibly under the impression that she is something edible. Both the young woman and the young man have mislaid their bathing suits. For further particulars see THE BISHOP'S JAEGERS.

convincing me he had the power to kill my Brownies. And he would do this whenever he wanted a quarter. Whereupon I would run through the house, crying, "They're dead! They're all dead!" until someone gave me a quarter which in turn I gave to my brother. He would then restore my Brownies to life while I, almost ill with anxiety, would welcome them back as from the grave. You can see by this that I was a very simple-minded child.

MR. YOUNG: "As the twig inclines the tree grows."

MR. SMITH: Insulting, but true. Those early experiences have left their mark with me. Even today I can see more vividly with my imagination than I can with my eyes. I don't quite side-step reality, but I'm inclined to read into it my own meanings; which is not always a wise thing to do. However, I'm just as happy as if I had real good sense. Don't you think this interview is getting a trifle long-winded?

MR. YOUNG: Yes, I think so. Why do you seem to do your best work while stripped to the buff and gleaming in the hot sun?

MR. SMITH: Because I like to write in hot countries, but I don't know what you mean by buff.

MR. YOUNG: Buff is merely an expression and not a biological term.

MR. SMITH: I feel greatly relieved.

MR. YOUNG: Is it because you like to write in hot countries that your women are so passionate?

MR. SMITH: No, they just get that way. I don't understand women very well who are not passionate.

16

MR. YOUNG: Your women are the kind that every man wants to meet every now and then, don't you think so?

MR. SMITH: Yes, Mr. Young. I'm afraid I think so. You mean that my women are both carnal and convivial and at the same time straight shooters. That to me is the ideal type.

MR. YOUNG: But your men, Mr. Smith. Do you consider them the kind that every woman wants to meet?

MR. SMITH: No. My men are rather rare characters and not so good-looking. To like them a woman must be endowed with a sense of humor and an inexhaustible fund of patience.

MR. YOUNG: Your women sort of pity them, I take it?

MR. SMITH: Most women pity men at one time or another.

MR. YOUNG: Why don't you write about great, strong silent men, Mr. Smith?

MR. SMITH: I don't believe there are any, unless they're too dumb to be interesting.

MR. YOUNG: Why do your women always pursue your men instead of the other way round?

MR. SMITH: The wish-complex. Then again in real life women usually know what they want much more definitely than men, and they are much more ruthless in getting what they want. Men seem to be born with conventional ideas. Had there been no fig leaves in the Garden Eve wouldn't have been greatly upset about it, whereas Adam would have made an awful fuss.

MR. YOUNG: I wouldn't have blamed him at all if he had. But you are not at all like Adam, Mr. Smith. You don't seem to mind what's on or off your body. Of course, with a body like yours it

17

doesn't really matter. Either clothed or nude it's just about as bad.

MR. SMITH: Be so good as to drag my body out of this interview.

MR. YOUNG: Willingly. To what do you ascribe the long life of your books? I don't think there's another author in America whose books are all in print and selling as well as when they were first published.

MR. SMITH: American madness, perhaps.

MR. YOUNG: But why has the madness attached itself solely to you?

MR. SMITH: I didn't know it had.

MR. YOUNG: How does it feel to be the founder of a cult?

MR. SMITH: By that you mean camp followers.

MR. YOUNG: In a manner of speaking. There are lots of authors trying to pull your stuff.

MR. SMITH: Then they're much madder than I am.

MR. YOUNG: Still, Mr. Smith, whether you like it or not, you have probably as great an influence on American morals as any writer now living. I hope you are thoroughly ashamed of yourself.

MR. SMITH: You speak like a publisher's blurb, Mr. Young. From what I've been observing during prohibition America has few morals left to be influenced.

MR. YOUNG: Is there any underlying philosophy in your novels, Mr. Smith?

MR. SMITH: I like people to read into my books their own meanings. They are always much better than the ones I intended.

MR. YOUNG: But your books must have some meaning, Mr. Smith.

18

MR. SMITH: The last paragraph in *The Night Life of the Gods* seems to have a little meaning.* I don't know. I don't like to talk about my books. It's more amusing to hear other people talk about them.

MR. YOUNG: Your readers get the impression that you are the sophisticated man-about-town type. Is there any justification for this?

MR. SMITH: Certainly my private life does not justify it. I am the least sought after author in America, if not the world. I know fewer so-called celebrities and go to fewer plays than any man I know outside a hospital. Interviewers find me both uninspiring and inarticulate. A little girl in the Middle West wrote me a letter about a child's book of mine called *Lazy Bear Lane.* That tickled me more than any letter I've ever received. I do a lot of window shopping with my wife. When I feel the need of an argument she is always ready to give me one. This holds true even when I don't feel the need. My eldest daughter is almost as big as her mother, which isn't saying much, and she gives me an argument, too. I've never had a room of my own to write in, and if I had I'd grow uneasy and begin to worry about what everyone else was doing. I do my best stuff while my wife and children and sisters-in-law are whispering piercingly across my desk. Most of the time the Smiths are on the trek either across some ocean

---

*"Yet through the deep silence of the vast hall something of them seemed to linger—Meg's last little sigh still floated like a mocking kiss on the cold cheek of convention."

(Several people have questioned Mr. Smith's opinion about this.)

or some continent. I'm a hard man for any woman to live with because I can do nothing at all with such an obvious air of complacency that I'd exasperate a saint.

MR. YOUNG: I think you're right. By the way, what did you think of Hollywood?

MR. SMITH: I thought a lot more about Hollywood than Hollywood thought about me, Mr. Young. I still carry the scars. They did everything to me out there but take me for a ride, and the reason they didn't do that was because they kept cutting my salary so that I wasn't worth the price of gasolene. It got so bad that I thought they were going to ask me to pay to get on the lot.

MR. YOUNG: Mr. Smith, as the interviewer I feel that I should have the last word. How about a Scotch and soda?

EDITOR'S NOTE

IN the course of the preceding interview Thorne Smith mentions one of his least known and most delightful books, LAZY BEAR LANE, a children's novel, that, like *Alice in Wonderland*, is equally interesting to grown-up readers. Filled with the gentle, bemused magic of all his work, tender and understanding, it tells the story of old Mr. and Mrs. Bingle, whom the enchantment of Lazy Bear brings back to youth again, to "all the lovely old lost things—the things we used to know."

Through the mazes of a bright new world Lazy Bear leads the two new-made children, into a Never-Never land that would have delighted Barrie, to make the acquaintanceship of Rudolph and Albert, the timid bears, of the woodland school for young deer, of all the strange and enchanting creatures that Thorne Smith's brilliant imagination conjures up so successfully. Perhaps it lies closer to the author's heart than any other of his books, for it was written first for his own two children. The pictures are by Edward Shanks, and one of them, showing Lazy Bear leading away the two gay children who were once sad old people, is reproduced below.

WHEREIN THE AUTHOR
IS PERMITTED TO SPEAK

BY THORNE SMITH

O ME IT IS ONLY TOO depressingly apparent that no one save myself is going to take this little effort of mine at all seriously. However, I am taking it quite seriously enough to make up for this lamentable lack of faith on the part of the passing reader.

Most people probably do not consider it a difficult thing to write a thousand or so odd words about oneself. In fact, to them the difficulty lies in writing less than a thousand words. But I consider it difficult. I consider it hellish. And this for the reason that those words have still to be written. They stretch endlessly before me like milestones along a weary way.

How to deal with them?

Well, in the first place, when an author starts in to write

about himself his chief preoccupation is to make himself appear whimsically modest and retiring in the eyes of the reader. Whimsical, by the way, and quizzical, are words that should be drummed out of the dictionary. But to return. When an author writes about himself he almost invariably endeavors craftily to conceal from the reader his monumental vanity and egotism.

I shall make no such humiliating concession.

Without so much as turning a hair I freely admit that I am one of America's greatest realists. And I'm not at all sure that this calm statement of facts does not take in all other nations, including the Scandinavian.

Like life itself my stories have no point and get absolutely nowhere. And like life they are a little mad and purposeless. They resemble those people who watch with placid concentration a steam shovel digging a large hole in the ground. They are almost as purposeless as a dignified commuter shaking an impotent fist after a train he has just missed. They are like the man who dashes madly through traffic only to linger aimlessly on the opposite corner watching a fountain pen being demonstrated in a shop window.

Quite casually I wander into my plot, poke around with my characters for a while, then amble off, leaving no moral proved and no reader improved.

The more I think about it the more am I convinced that I'm a trifle cosmic. My books are as blindly unreasonable as nature. They have no more justification than a tiresomely high mountain or a garrulous and untidy volcano. Unlike the great idealists and romancers who insist on a beginning and a middle and an ending for their stories mine possess none of these definite parts. You can open them at any page. It does not matter at all. You will be equally mystified if not revolted. I am myself.

Many eons ago when I first slithered from the primeval slime with a merry band of reptiles I sat down on the relatively dry land and dashed off a series of sonnet things which I considered well above the average. It was at that time that I formed the determination to become a poet. As a matter of fact I realized I was a poet already, but I meant to make all the other reptiles admit it.

Some years later when I was a very small boy this determination found expression. In those days I used to occupy a huge bed with my even smaller cousin, Almerine. And to this bed would come on furtive, guilty feet a great black dog who called himself Zeb. He would shoulder himself beneath the covers then thrust out his massive legs. My cousin and myself would be unceremoniously shoved against the wall while Zeb with a sigh of sheer exhaustion fell heavily asleep. We permitted the dog to have most of the bed because we realized as only children can how much he had to contend with during the day, how difficult was his life and what unpleasant names he was called.

It was to this audience, the slumbering beast and my small cousin—that I told my first stories and recited my first poems until presently the three of us were asleep.

Night after night this continued until I bade farewell to dog, bed and little cousin in North Carolina and went to boarding school in Virginia.

Here I found myself wandering round the cow sheds and singing in a quavering voice, "God Be With You 'Till We Meet Again," which goes to show that to my poetic frenzy had been added a deep religious under-current picked up from the darkies and lost later somewhere along the road. With a broken heart I was making the air hideous even for the cows, because of a clean little girl with golden curls I had met and lost at a strawberry festival.

She was about the cleanest little girl I can remember ever having seen; and now that I have two little girls of my own I wonder from time to time how that little girl ever managed to get herself so clean. It was appalling. I could soak my own two children in a tub for weeks and still find smudges on them somewhere when eventually I dragged them out.

It was at this period that I abandoned poetry for a while in favor of music as revealed to me through the sobbing notes of a harmonica, much more aptly termed a mouth organ. Even at this moment I lay claim to being the most realistic amateur harmonica player in America.

For years a certain gentleman of letters who lurks behind the initials of F. P. A. has been making wild statements about his ability to play on this instrument. I am so good I let them pass. To me such unfounded confidence is amusing. I learned the harmonica from a race for which it was born, and I worked for hours picking beans to earn the money with which to buy my first one. It had a horn on it. And I walked eighteen miles to get the thing.

My first poem was printed in the *New York Herald*. It was a scoffing poem about the then Secretary of the Navy. My father, a naval officer himself, apparently shared my views for he sent me twenty-five dollars. The *New York Herald* sent me nothing.

Some years later the old established publishing house of Frederick Stokes & Company suddenly went mad, and published a book of my verse, the entire edition of which I wish I had back right now for purposes of destruction. In spite of which I have had another book of verse ready for years. Every week I bring it to my publishers and mutely offer it to them only to be told that on that particular day they are not taking any verse no matter how bad. They are nice about it but firm, which is a fortunate thing for me as well as the unwary public.

I became an author by invitation. It was not my fault. I will admit it was my fault that I continued to be an author, but the first crime was not of my contrivance. It was during the war. A character I had been writing about in a service magazine I was editing appealed to this same house of Stokes. All I did was to clip my stuff from the back issues, and lo, I became an author. By this simple method I became an author twice. After that things were not so easy. I soon learned how it felt to be despised and rejected.

Topper, my first novel, started out to be a short story. My wife needed clothes so that she could appear covered if not clad in public. After I had had done the first ten pages I suddenly realized I had written a swell first chapter for a

This, in case you don't recognise it, is a whale. Why it is mounted on wheels and what the lady and gentlemen plan to do with it is a problem to which only RAIN IN THE DOORWAY can offer a solution.

book. I told this to my wife. She sighed and went back to bed. Some months later I bought her a frock of sorts and she sallied forth to see what changes had taken place in the city during her enforced absence from it.

In *Topper* there is a dog called Oscar, and on the lawn of my one-acre estate there is the tallest, wildest grass in all the world. Once I saw the tail of a dog progressing through this grass like a periscope through the waves. This quaint spectacle set me to thinking about a tail without a dog, and a dog without a tail, and legs without a body, and a body without legs and all sorts of odd manifestations. Thus Oscar came into being. I still like him and wish him well.

Dream's End, my first serious novel, done years ago, is considered by many my funniest. I don't speak to these people, though.

The idea for *The Stray Lamb* struck me in the middle of heavy traffic while crossing Fifth Avenue. An officer flung me from his sight, telling me never to cross his part of the Avenue

27

again as long as either of us lived. I sneaked past him the next day.

For several years I had to live with the idea of *The Stray Lamb* buzzing in my brain before I could find a publisher generous enough to enable me to write it. To Joe Anthony of the defunct Cosmopolitan Book Corporation I shall be eternally grateful. Those were mean, bad years, those years between *Dream's End* and *The Stray Lamb*. And the big bad wolf was seldom very far from my run down heels. I did have a publisher then, but—oh well, why bring up the past.

It was not until my present publishers suffered me to come unto them that I began to write with any degree of confidence and regularity. In me they instinctively recognized the great American realist as well as an author possessing the ability to disappear most amazingly and disconcertingly at the wrong times. They have been patient with me about this and discounted my bad ways. But they are firm about not publishing my poems. I hope I don't break them down.

It is an odd thing that for many years before I got to know Roland Young, who appears in fragments up front in this booklet, I was an intelligent admirer of his works on the stage. He is more than all right there, but in an earthquake he gets quaint ideas. During the last big one in Southern California he seemed to feel that people were interested in the effect of the quake on his gold fish. Both of us were in Hollywood at the time, and he kept calling me up to tell me that his confounded goldfish were being washed up against his windows. As if I cared. A goldfish means less to me in an earthquake than a snap of my fingers. It didn't matter to me if his fish were washed down his gullet. I was too busy with the quake and had scant time for his foolish fish. But I was too much of a gentleman to tell him so.

Actors are like that. They are not sensible like great American realists.

So this is about all. My favorite hobbies are fountain pens, safety razors and not hearing Roland Young talk about goldfish during an earthquake. I also have a fondness for billiards, which I do not play. My chief recreation is making appointments to give little talks and then going away somewhere else. This has greatly endeared me to my publishers.

The words have at last been written. I come to an abrupt end.

A COMPLETE BIBLIOGRAPHY OF
THORNE SMITH'S WORK

1918: BILTMORE OSWALD: *The Diary of a Hapless Recruit.*
Illustrated by Richard Dorgan. (by J. Thorne Smith,
Jr., U.S.N.R.F.) New York, Frederick A. Stokes
Company. (Reprinted from *The Broadside*, a Journal
for the Naval Reserve Force.)

1919: OUT O' LUCK: *Biltmore Oswald Very Much at Sea.*
Illustrated by Richard Dorgan. (by J. Thorne Smith,
Jr., C.B.M., U.S.N.R.F.) New York, Frederick A.
Stokes Company. (Reprinted from *The Broadside*,
a Journal for the Naval Reserve Force).
HAUNTS AND BYPATHS AND OTHER POEMS. New York,
Frederick A. Stokes Company

1921: CIVILIZATION IN THE UNITED STATES (A symposium
containing chapters by Thorne Smith and thirty-two
other contributors). New York, Harcourt Brace &
Company

1926: TOPPER: *An Improbable Adventure.* New York, Robert M.
McBride & Company
TOPPER: *An Improbable Adventure.* London, Robert
Holden

1927: DREAM'S END. New York, Robert M. McBride &
Company

1928: DREAM'S END. London, Jarrolds, Ltd., Publishers.

1929: THE STRAY LAMB. New York, Cosmopolitan Book Corporation.

1930: THE STRAY LAMB. London, William Heinemann, Ltd. DID SHE FALL?, New York, Cosmopolitan Book Corporation.

1931

March: THE NIGHT LIFE OF THE GODS. New York, Doubleday, Doran & Company.

September: TURNABOUT. New York, Doubleday, Doran & Company.

November: LAZY BEAR LANE (juvenile). New York, Doubleday, Doran & Company.

1932

May: TOPPER TAKES A TRIP. Illustrated by Herbert Roese. New York, Doubleday, Doran & Company.

June: DID SHE FALL? (first Doubleday, Doran edition). New York, Doubleday, Doran & Company.

September: THE STRAY LAMB (first Doubleday, Doran edition). New York, Doubleday, Doran & Company.

October: THE BISHOP'S JAEGERS. Illustrated by Herbert Roese. New York, Doubleday, Doran & Company.

1933

January: THE JOVIAL GHOSTS (*Topper*). London, Arthur Barker, Ltd.
RAIN IN THE DOORWAY. Illustrated by Herbert Roese. New York, Doubleday, Doran & Company.
TOPPER (reprint edition—large 12mo.— $1.00), New York, Grosset & Dunlap.

TOPPER (reprint edition—12mo.—75c), New York, Grosset & Dunlap.

September: TURNABOUT. London, Arthur Barker, Ltd.

December: SKIN AND BONES. Illustrated by Herbert Roese. New York, Doubleday, Doran & Company.

1934

January: THE NIGHT LIFE OF THE GODS. London. Arthur Barker, Ltd.

February: YONDER'S HENRY (short story). *Esquire*, Vol. I No. 3.

THE ILLUSTRATOR

HERE AND THERE in the preceding pages will be found a variety of illustrations. With three exceptions (the portrait of Mr. Smith and the handsome drawing of a flea are both by Roland Young) they are the products of Herbert Roese's inspired pen, and are taken from several of Thorne Smith's books. Explanations are supplied with most of them, except those which obscure the initial letters here and there. These are taken from SKIN AND BONES, and it wouldn't do any good to try and explain them, because the whole of SKIN AND BONES is hardly sufficient to do that.

With the course of years Mr. Roese has become as closely identified with Mr. Smith as ever Tenniel was with Lewis Carroll. His pictures have mirrored the text with such unblushing fidelity that today a new Smith novel without his pictures would be unthinkable.

Breinigsville, PA USA
12 April 2010
235985BV00005B/28/P

9 781593 935283